# Promoting the Gift of Literacy

*101 Lesson Plans*
*for Oral and Written Language*

## Rhea A. Ashmore

*University of Montana*

## Allyn and Bacon

BOSTON ▪ LONDON ▪ TORONTO ▪ SYDNEY ▪ TOKYO ▪ SINGAPORE

*Series editor:* Arnis E. Burvikovs
*Series editorial assistant:* Patrice Mailloux
*Marketing manager:* Kathleen Morgan

**Library of Congress Cataloging-in-Publication Data**

Ashmore, Rhea A.
  Promoting the gift of literacy : 101 lesson plans for oral and written language /
Rhea A. Ashmore.
      p.   cm.
    Includes bibliographical references and index.
    ISBN 0-205-30864-3
    1. Language arts (Elementary)—United States.   2. Oral communication—Study and teaching (Elementary)—United States.   3. Lesson planning—United States.   I. Title.

LB1576 .A717 2001
372.6'044—dc21                                                              00-058273

Printed in the United States of America
10  9  8  7  6  5  4  3  2  1      04  03  02  01  00

To John, Johnny, Giovanni, Juan, Jashu, Guido,
Jan, and Larry, with many thanks.

*Rheann*

# Contents

# *Preface and Acknowledgments*

Literacy is a treasure that follows its owner everywhere. *Promoting the Gift of Literacy: 101 Lesson Plans for Oral and Written Language* is an essential book for enhancing literacy learning. Pre-service teachers, paraprofessionals, tutors, classroom professionals, specialized reading professionals, allied professionals, and, most important, parents and caregivers are provided comprehensive lesson plans. The plans are leveled according to three literacy stages: initial reading, transitional, and basic literacy. This supports literacy learning as a complex process involving more than chronological age or grade levels. The plans also include intended learning outcomes, materials, and activities in four literacy domains: (1) oral and written language, (2) word recognition, (3) comprehension and strategic reading for narrative text, and (4) study skills and strategic reading for content area text. In turn, the learners, whatever their ages, are engaged in a variety of appropriate literacy activities.

The lesson plans are comprehensive; one does not need to thumb through the text to find information. Per lesson plan, relevant activity forms are included, full references are cited, and other recommended books are noted (substituting books based on the interests and abilities of the reader is recommended). The pages are perforated and three-hole punched, ready for lamination and/or organizational purposes.

There are 100 detailed lesson plans, 25 per domain. The 101st domain is blank; the reader is encouraged to use this template for further lesson planning. The premise of the book is that literacy learning is a language-based process that is best acquired through functional, pragmatic activities.

The appendixes contain information that serves as a primary resource and reference tool. Included are Appendix A: the literacy lesson plan template; Appendix B: a list of award-winning books; Appendix C: literature cited in the lesson plans; Appendix D: professional resources; and Appendix E: Internet sites related to literacy.

My purpose in writing this book is to support literacy. As a child, I developed the gift of literacy thanks to my parents and dedicated teachers. I recall the joy of reading aloud to my mother as she curled my hair, and my early lessons with Mrs. Kennedy, my first-grade teacher, who integrated reading with art. As an educator for more than 30 years, I have witnessed the joy of extending this gift to both children and adults. Now the opportunity is yours.

## ACKNOWLEDGMENTS

This work was supported in part by the Montana Early Literacy Grant (#H024B9600034). Thanks to the undergraduate and graduate students who contributed to the development of this book: Susan Asanovich, Marsha Badger, Kathleen Bahnson, Jamie Beierle, Susannah Bletner, Patricia Boncz, Liza Britton, Emily Brockman, Dawn Darrow, Jennifer Decker, Rose Dehne, Lisa Huckins, Rebecca Jay, Chris Johnson, Melissa Johnson, Kevin Keegan, Grace Mears, Robert Miller, Matt Porrovecchio, Nanci Reed, Maer Rubley, Carole Schletz, Joyce Singleton, Sara Taes, Jill Thelen, Sharon Wilson, and Bert Wittl. Appreciation is extended to Douglas Ita, John Lazarowicz, and Cynthia Manning for their thoughtful proofreading. Special thanks to the following individuals who reviewed the book for Allyn and Bacon: Lorraine Gerstl, Santa Cataling, and Eileen Madaus, Newton Public Schools. Your comments were most insightful and useful. In addition, here's to the production staff at Allyn and Bacon, including Bridget Keane, Patrice Mailloux, Elana Parente, and particularly Virginia Lanigan, senior editor, who guided me through the initial stages of writing this book, and Arnis E. Burvikovs, editor, who assisted me to the finish line.

# Promoting the Gift of Literacy

*Part One*

# Foundations

■ ■ ■ ■

---

Real reading is still the noblest of the arts, the medium by which
there still come to us the loftiest inspirations, the highest ideals,
the purest feelings that have been allowed mankind,—a God-gift
indeed, this written word and the power to interpret it.

—E. B. Huey,
*The Psychology and Pedagogy of Reading*, p. 5

CHAPTER 1

*Literacy and
the Domains*

Crystal, age 12, lived with her mother and three older brothers and was in grade 7 in an urban middle school. An attentive and well-mannered child, she seemed small for her age and did not read as well as her peers. Cultural deprivation offered at least a partial explanation for Crystal's meager vocabulary and limited experience. Her physical examination revealed no visual, auditory, or neurological handicapping factors.

When Crystal's teacher, Mr. Jones, enrolled in a diagnosis of reading and writing course at a nearby institution of higher learning, he needed a subject for a case study with whom to work for the semester. He chose Crystal.

While she was in grade 6, Crystal's former teacher administered a group intelligence test to the class. Because the contents were highly verbal, Mr. Jones suspected that Crystal's reported IQ score of 88 was unreliable. Therefore, Mr. Jones arranged for Crystal to be tested by the school psychologist.

Crystal was administered a standardized individual intelligence test. On this measure, she obtained a Verbal IQ score of 93, a Performance IQ score of 115, and a resulting Full Scale score of 104. The 22-point discrepancy between her Verbal and Performance IQ scores indicated much stronger nonverbal than verbal skills. Her strengths on this instrument were perceptual organization and attention to details, visual sequencing, and spatial relations. Her weaknesses were related to her general fund of information and arithmetic skills.

Mr. Jones also administered several informal assessments. First, the results of an informal reading inventory indicated independent reading (ability to

3

process print without assistance) at level 3, instructional reading (ability to process print with assistance) at levels 4–5, and frustration reading (inability to process print with or without assistance) at level 6. Her listening comprehension was at level 7. Crystal read in a slow and halting fashion, making a number of repetitions and substitutions: "interpret" for *interrupt*, "plants" for *planet*, and "fraction" for *friction*. Regarding oral reading comprehension, she had difficulty answering cause-and-effect, inference, and detail questions. Her listening comprehension level suggested that she comprehended material read to her at higher levels than she could read by herself with understanding.

Completion of a reading attitude survey suggested a somewhat positive attitude toward reading. An interest interview indicated that Crystal enjoyed horses, sports, and books about relationships. Finally, when Mr. Jones asked Crystal to write a paragraph of her choice, she wrote about a recent field trip to the zoo. Her handwriting was legible, an organization pattern was evident, and ideas were presented in a logical order. However, the topic sentence was confusing, many words were misspelled, and punctuation was lacking.

If Crystal were your case study subject or student or child, what would you do to develop her literacy skills? A good place to start is to ask the following questions: What is reading? What is literacy? How does one plan for effective literacy instruction based on the learner's literacy strengths and needs? Asking reflective questions is critical to literacy instruction. First, one must develop personal beliefs about literacy and learning in order to make decisions about what to teach and how best to teach it. Next, one must plan for instruction.

Let us begin by exploring some definitions of reading:

> For me, reading is a transaction that takes place between a reader and a text in a particular situation. The reader constructs meaning by actively processing graphic, syntactic, and semantic cues representing language, and by actively using memories of past experiences to aid in building new thoughts and/or revising, reinforcing, or expanding current thoughts. (Gipe, 1998, p. 13)

> I define reading as a message-getting, problem-solving activity which increases in power and flexibility the more it is practiced. My definition states that within the directional constraints of the printer's code, language and visual perception responses are purposefully directed by the reader in some integrated way to the problem of extracting meaning from cues in a text, in sequence, so that the reader brings a maximum of understanding to the author's message. (Clay, 1991, p. 6)

> Reading is a social, developmental, and interactive process that involves learning. It is a process incorporating a person's linguistic knowledge that can be powerfully influenced by an insightful teacher as well as other nonlinguistic internal and external conditions. It can be developed by self-directed learning experiences as well as by direct instruction and is increasingly important in the information age in which we live. (Leu & Kinzer, 1999, p. 11)

> Reading is a complex developmental challenge that we know to be intertwined with many other developmental accomplishments: attention, memory, language, and motivation, for example. Reading is not only a cognitive psycholinguistic activity but also a social activity. (Snow, Burns, & Griffin, 1998, p. 15)

Several implications emerge from these definitions of reading. Reflecting on these aspects contributes to one's philosophy of reading and sets the foundation for effective literacy instruction:

1. Reading is a developmental process that begins at home in the early years.
2. Reading is a cognitive process or one that refers to the nature of knowing.
3. Reading is a social process that reflects not only the reader's knowledge but also one's particular attitudes and concerns and environmental conditions.
4. Reading is an emerging language process that intertwines with the writing process.
5. Reading is enhanced when a variety of approaches, strategies, and materials are used.
6. The more one reads, the better one reads.

How does one define literacy? As the reading process is a complex one, in this book the terms *reading* and *literacy* are used interchangeably. Indeed, the intimate connections among reading, writing, listening, and speaking are well documented. Braunger and Lewis (1997) state the following:

> Research in the field may focus on one mode of literacy development—for example, reading—but an important lesson of recent research in reading has been that all forms of language and literacy develop supportively and interactively. Children build upon oral language knowledge and strategies as they learn to read and write; they develop key understandings about reading—especially phonics—through writing, and they extend their writing range through reading. (p. 1)

What are the characteristics of an effective literacy lesson? The definitions of reading and literacy support instruction by means of a variety of activities with an assortment of materials at all levels of education. And literacy abilities are interrelated; growth in one area aids growth in another. For purposes of assessment and lesson design, although these abilities are interconnected, they require categorization. *Standards for Reading Professionals* (Professional Standards and Ethics Committee, 1998), a publication that assists in the establishment and evaluation of teacher preparation programs, includes the following under instruction and assessment: word identification, vocabulary, and spelling; comprehension; study strategies; and writing.

Adapted from this model, the lesson plans in Part Two are categorized in four major domains: (1) oral and written language, (2) word recognition, (3) comprehension and strategic reading for narrative text, and (4) study skills and strategic reading for content area text. Following each domain, the area of instruction is identified (e.g., oral and written language: creative writing). Area identification provides a focus for instruction.

## ORAL AND WRITTEN LANGUAGE

Oral and written language ability is at the core of the reading process. Research studies demonstrate the power of early preschool language to predict reading ability three to five years later (Scarborough, 1991; Shapiro et al., 1990; Walker, Greenwood, Hart, & Carta, 1994). Likewise, reading and writing are inseparable processes, and written language activities provide opportunities to explore the various uses and functions of written language and develop appreciation and command of them. Examples of oral and written language activities include:

- Adult–child shared book reading that stimulates verbal interaction to enhance language development and knowledge about print concepts
- Activities that direct young children's attention to the phonological structure of spoken words (e.g., games, songs, and poems that emphasize rhyming or manipulation of sounds)
- Activities that highlight the relations between print and speech
- Understanding and application of the writing process (brainstorming ideas, organizing thoughts, writing a first draft, revising, editing, and proofreading)
- Knowledge and application of the conventions of standard written English

## WORD RECOGNITION

Word recognition involves learning about sounds and letters and using print for meaning. Activities in phonics, sight words, vocabulary, fluency, structural analysis, and use of context clues support the domain of word recognition.

A variety of teaching approaches to word recognition lessons are recommended. Explicit or direct instruction that guides the reader's attention to the sound structure of language and to the connections between speech sounds and spellings assists the student in learning specific word identification skills. As well, implicit instruction that integrates skill components promotes literacy learning in the context of meaningful activities based on the reader's interests and on quality literature. Rather than debate which approach is better, use both.

## COMPREHENSION AND STRATEGIC READING FOR NARRATIVE TEXT

Reading is an active, cognitive, and affective process in which the reader actively engages with the text and builds her own understanding of it. This is comprehension. Instruction should include explicitly taught comprehension strategies for reading narrative (literature) as well as expository text (content area text). Regarding the lesson plans in this book, two domains accommodate this differentiation: (1) comprehension and strategic reading for narrative text and (2) study skills and strategic reading for content area text.

To explain reading comprehension in more detail, Davis (1944) cited nine skills considered basic to successful comprehension:

1. Knowledge of word meanings
2. Ability to select appropriate meaning for a word or phrase in the light of its particular contextual setting
3. Ability to follow the organization of a passage and to identify antecedents and references in it
4. Ability to identify the main thought of a passage
5. Ability to answer questions that are specifically answered in a passage
6. Ability to answer questions that are answered in a passage, but not in the words in which the question is asked
7. Ability to draw inferences from a passage about its contents
8. Ability to recognize the literary devices used in a passage and to determine its tone and mood
9. Ability to determine a writer's purpose, intent, and point of view, that is, to draw inferences about a writer. (p. 186)

The lesson plans presented in this domain take in these comprehension skills.

## STUDY SKILLS AND STRATEGIC READING FOR CONTENT AREA TEXT

Study skills are learned abilities for extending knowledge and competence. They include work-study skills (alphabetizing, knowledge of book parts, use of reference materials), organizing information (finding main ideas, sequencing, note-taking), and interpreting graphic and pictorial materials (pictures, tables and charts, maps and globes). Study skills augment the learner's underlying knowledge and competencies in the domains of oral and written language, word recognition, and comprehension.

Study skills are taught and used with expository text or materials that explain. These are content area textbooks and other informative materials that are usually introduced after the primary years of elementary education. Explicit teaching of study skills should accompany these materials. Otherwise, the student who is a good reader may not know how to deal with the wide range of textbooks and assignments.

Let's return to the vignette about Crystal and apply it to literacy instruction. An effective way to do this is to ask four correlative diagnostic questions (Gipe, 1998):

1. Does Crystal have a reading need(s)? Yes.
2. In what domain(s) is the need? Comprehension and strategic reading for narrative text is an obvious domain. Crystal had difficulty answering cause-and-effect, inference, and detail questions, and she made substitutions that did not make sense.
3. In what area of the domain is the need? Considering the nine skills in reading comprehension (Davis, 1944), Crystal requires instruction in several areas. Because she made substitutions, the facilitator of literacy decides to start with the area of context clues.
4. What literacy lesson will be devised and taught? The answer to this question is presented in Chapter 2.

CHAPTER *2*

# *The Literacy Lesson Plan Format*

Once the domain and area of instruction have been identified, the facilitator of literacy designs a lesson plan. Lesson plans come in a variety of formats; however, good lesson plans contain three critical components: instructional objectives or intended learning outcomes; materials; and activities that prepare, guide, reinforce, and assess whether the learner has achieved the outcome.

The literacy lessons presented in Part Two are structured as shown in Figure 2-1. To avoid ambiguity and provide uniformity in the content of the lesson plans, the traditional terms *teacher* and *student* are used. The pronouns *he* and *she* alternate in the lesson plans when referring to students. Feel free to substitute your name for "teacher" and the learner's name for "student."

The first literacy lesson section is **domain and area of instruction;** for example, Comprehension and Strategic Reading for Narrative Text: Context Clues. Chapters 3–6 are arranged based on the following domains: oral and written language, word recognition, comprehension and strategic reading for narrative text, and study skills and strategic reading for content area text. To facilitate identification, the first letter is the initial that corresponds to the domain:

 for oral and written language,

 for word recognition,

for comprehension and strategic reading for narrative text, and

for study skills and strategic reading for content area text.

Following each domain is the area. The area identifies the level of specificity for instruction. It is important to remember that reading is a process and that the domains and areas are interrelated. By focusing on a specific domain and area, the instructor makes a choice about what to teach from the vast amount of content possible.

Included in the domain and area of instruction is the literacy stage of development. The literacy stages of **initial reading**, **transitional**, and **basic literacy** portray that literacy learning is a continuous process that involves more than chronological age or grade levels. For example, an adult who has been identified with significant reading needs may require lessons at the initial reading stage.

Initial reading describes learners who can identify specific words in their printed form, such as names, labels, sight words, and high meaning words, and who can decode orthographically regular multisyllable words and nonsense words (e.g., *capital*, *zot*). The writing process is characterized by sensitivity to conventional spelling and use of invented spelling based on phonics knowledge. The learner composes fairly readable first drafts using appropriate parts of the writing process, such as planning, drafting, rereading for meaning, and some self-correction. The majority of children experience initial reading during grades 1 and 2.

Learners who use letter-sound correspondence knowledge and structural analysis to decode print but are not yet fluent readers are in the transitional

Domain and Area of Instruction

Intended Learning Outcome

Materials

Prereading Activity

Reading Activity

Postreading Activity

Independent Practice

Suggested Reading and/or Notes

**Figure 2-1.**    Literacy lesson plan format.

stage. They read and comprehend both fiction and nonfiction that is appropriately designed for their levels. They correctly spell previously studied words and produce a variety of written works (e.g., letters, reports, journal writing). They begin to use study skills in their content area readings. Most children experience the transitional stage in grades 2–5. Considering Crystal's reading strengths and needs, she is in the transitional stage.

Basic literacy consists of refinement of literacy competencies. Vocabulary continues to expand, reading fluency increases, higher-level thinking and reasoning competencies develop, and study skills use continues. The writing process develops as students combine information from multiple sources in writing reports, edit and revise their own writing as well as respond to others' compositions, and use all aspects of the writing process in producing compositions and reports. Most learners enter this stage in grade 6 or 7 and continue to refine their literacy skills throughout their lives.

The second literacy lesson section states the **intended learning outcome**. This is similar to an instructional objective or a performance objective. It is the desired outcome of learning, expressed in terms of observable behavior or performance of the learner. According to Montague (1987), an intended learning outcome contains three components: (1) a verb defining some observable action, (2) a description of the task to be performed, and (3) a criterion to judge if the learner performed the task satisfactorily.

Here are three examples of intended learning outcomes from the literacy lesson plans:

1. The student will write a five-item shopping list and purchase the items under supervision with 100 percent accuracy.
2. Given a teacher-made cloze worksheet based on the selected book, the student will fill in the blanks with 50 percent accuracy.
3. Given five random events from a chapter in the book *Charlotte's Web* (White, 1952), the student will order them in sequence with 100 percent accuracy.

In the first example, the observable verb is *will write*, the description of the task is the entire wording of the outcome, and the criterion is *100 percent*. In the second example, the observable verb is *will fill*, the description of the task is encompassed in the entire wording, and the criterion is *50 percent*. In the final example, the observable verb is *will order*; the description of the task is described in the entire wording, and the criterion is *100 percent*. An effective way to assess the completeness of the intended learning outcome is to read it and then ask, "If I were a substitute teacher, would I know what to do and expect of the student?"

The third section is **materials**. The resources necessary to implement the lesson are listed. This is similar to gathering the ingredients for a recipe. One should have the appropriate resources to support instruction and to provide a variety of ways for students to connect their experiences to the lesson. Maintaining a list of resources saves time and prepares a teacher for both present and future instruction.

The subsequent sections of the lesson plan describe the various activities. The **prereading activity** is the focusing event or "hook" that activates prior knowledge and excites the learner to participate. Activities should encourage the student to consider what she already knows about the topic and to clarify a specific purpose for reading. In addition, the teacher can explicitly demonstrate the acquired knowledge or skill through modeling. As some students learn more efficiently by copying the behavior of another, modeling allows the learner to witness and imitate the role model who explains and performs the finished product.

Prereading activities should involve the learner in as many ways and through as many senses as possible. This takes into consideration the several intelligences introduced by Howard Gardner in *Frames of Mind* (1983) and expanded on in *MI: Intelligence, Understanding, and the Mind* (video, 1996). The following briefly describes the multiple intelligences (MI):

*Linguistic intelligence.*   This is the capacity to use words effectively, whether orally (as a storyteller, orator, or politician) or in writing (as a poet, editor, or journalist). This intelligence includes the ability to use the syntax or structure of language, the phonology or sounds of language, the semantics or meanings of language, and the practical uses of language. Literacy and linguistic intelligence are interconnected.

*Logical-mathematical intelligence.*   This is the capacity to use numbers effectively (as a mathematician or statistician) and to reason well (as a scientist or computer programmer). This intelligence includes sensitivity to logical patterns and relationships, statements and propositions (if-then, cause-effect), functions, and other related abstractions.

*Spatial intelligence.*   This is the ability to perceive the visual-spatial world accurately (as a sculptor or painter) and to perform transformations on those perceptions (as an architect, artist, or inventor). The intelligence involves sensitivity to color, line, shape, form, space, and the relationships among these elements.

*Bodily-kinesthetic intelligence.*   This is expertise in using one's whole body to express ideas and feelings (such as an actor, dancer, or athlete) and facility in using one's hands to produce or transform things (such as a mechanic, surgeon, or sculptor). This intelligence includes physical skills such as coordination, balance, dexterity, strength, flexibility, and speed.

*Musical intelligence.*   This is the capacity to perceive, discriminate, transform, and express musical forms (such as a music aficionado, a music critic, a composer, or performer). This intelligence includes sensitivity to rhythm, pitch, melody, and tone.

*Interpersonal intelligence.*    This is the ability to perceive and make distinctions in the moods, intentions, motivations, and feelings of other people (such as a counselor, teacher, or politician). This intelligence includes sensitivity to facial expressions, voice, and gestures and the ability to respond effectively to those cues, such as influencing a group of people to follow a certain line of action.

*Intrapersonal intelligence.*    This is self-knowledge and the ability to act adaptively on the basis of that knowledge (such as a therapist or social worker). This intelligence includes self-understanding and an awareness of inner moods, intentions, motivations, desires, self-discipline, and self-esteem.

*Naturalistic intelligence.*    This is awareness of nature and the ability to adapt to the outdoors (such as a sailor, trekker, or hunter). This intelligence includes orientation skills and the ability to adapt and survive in nature's elements.

The MI theory suggests that facilitators of literacy integrate linguistic lessons with activities that represent a student's demonstrated intelligences. Rather than assigning a reading selection, lecturing in the front of the classroom, and writing on the board, teachers shift their method of presentation from linguistic to spatial to musical and so on, often combining teaching strategies based on intelligences in creative ways.

The **reading activity** describes what will be read and how it will be read. Regarding what will be read, the possibilities are legion: folk literature, fantasy literature, realistic fiction, nonfiction literature, poetic compositions, books with pictures, best-sellers, textbooks, student-made books, letters, the newspaper, and information on the Internet. The reading material selected is dependent on the school's curriculum guides, adopted textbooks, and the myriad sources of materials that successful facilitators of literacy use to bring life to literacy lessons.

Reading occurs in a variety of ways. Reading aloud to children promotes the premise that reading is enjoyable, print is related to spoken language, and stories have predictable structure. Readers Theatre (Sloyer, 1982) engages a group of readers in a dramatic presentation of a short script adapted from a reading selection. Drop Everything And Read (DEAR) (McCracken, 1971) and Sustained Silent Reading (SSR) provide uninterrupted time for both teachers and students to read self-selected materials silently. In echo reading (Walker, 1992), the teacher reads one sentence of text aloud with appropriate intonation and phrasing, and the student imitates the oral reading model.

Skimming and scanning promote flexibility in rate of reading and reading for main ideas and specific information. Many ways abound to read both silently and orally.

The **postreading activity** is the closing of the lesson if the teacher is present. He should restate and reinforce the important generalizations learned from the lesson. Also, regarding assessment, the intended learning outcome is assessed here.

Assessment is decision making based on gathering information and evaluating the information about the learner. According to Orlich, Harder, Callahan, and Gibson (1998):

> Assessment, the most general term, includes a broad range of processes by which teachers gather information about student learning. These processes include paper-and-pencil tests, performance and project ratings, and observations. Assessment is in part a qualitative description—making a value judgment in response to the question "How well does the student perform?" (p. 353)

Assessment provides data for reexamination of literacy behaviors. Did the student reach or surpass the criterion in the intended learning outcome? If yes, a new lesson can be devised. If no, further instruction is necessary. The instructional cycle continues as the teacher gathers information, evaluates the information, and generates further instructional plans for the learner.

When literature is used in a literacy lesson plan, the opportunity for authentic assessment occurs. This involves observing the individual as she is reading and responding to literature, examining the work she produces as part of her reading and responding, and discussing with the reader what she is doing. It also involves assessing yourself as a facilitator of literacy: your planning, your interaction, and your flexibility.

Do authentic assessment by keeping records and collecting readers' work, observing behaviors, and listening. Ask your student to maintain an ongoing reading log or journal that lists what she reads and her reactions to it. Observe your reader as she selects books and reads and responds to the content. Are the selections appropriate to the individual's strengths and needs? When reading, does she focus on meaning or solely on pronouncing words? Who does she read with, and where does she like to read? As you observe the reader, write down brief anecdotes.

Listen to the reader as she discusses books and reading. Note her ideas and whether she attends to others' ideas. Have your student compile her unique portfolio reflecting what she learned about literacy and through literacy. Cullinan and Galda (1998) recommend the following for students:

1. Ask students to keep samples of their work in portfolios. Record the date on each piece. Periodically review samples with students and decide together what to keep for parent conferences or for their cumu-

lative file. Ask students what they are learning and what would reflect that learning. Ask what else they feel they need to learn. Write your assessment of what they do well and what they need to work toward. Each student does the same.

2. Have students discuss in small groups what they are learning.
3. Ask students to keep a log of what they read.
4. Ask students to keep journals about their reading.
5. Keep samples of the ways students respond to what they read.

For teachers, they recommend the following:

1. Summarize the genres that students read.
2. Summarize the list of favorite authors that students read.
3. Examine what your students discuss about the books they read (plot, character, language, theme).
4. Notice how your students relate what they are reading to things they have read previously.
5. Observe how students select books: Do they select ones they can read? Ones that provide information they need? (p. 408)

A traditional term for **independent practice** is *homework*. Lessons should promote independent reading outside the school setting by such means as daily at-home reading assignments and expectations, summer reading lists, encouragement of parent involvement, and work with community groups, including public librarians, who share this goal (Snow et al., 1998). Studies demonstrate that memory is enhanced when information is presented at the beginning and ending of a lesson (Armento, 1977; Wright & Nuthall, 1970). Therefore, inform students of their assignments at least twice per lesson.

Independent practice requires the student to work on her own. Opportunities for this activity occur in the classroom, during study periods, or outside of the school setting. If independent practice takes place in the classroom, the teacher should circulate among the students, checking to ensure that students are reinforcing learning rather than practicing mistakes. In addition, depending on the assignment, there should be some way for students to check their results as they proceed independently.

Independent practice that occurs outside the classroom requires the student to practice a skill or behavior without teacher guidance. Involving family members, caregivers, or friends in the assignment makes it more relevant and based on real-life learning, while it also provides informal supervision.

The terms *unitization phase* and *automaticity* describe the two stages that occur during independent practice (Samuels, 1981). *Unitization* means attending carefully to the new skill or behavior, working slowly and with effort. On reaching automaticity, the student works more quickly and responds automatically as the skill or performance is overlearned through practice and repetition. Gunter, Estes, and Schwab (1990) state:

Homework is most effective when students have reached unitization of learning but have not yet reached automaticity. As the most frequently used form of independent practice, homework is often abused by sending children home to practice material before they understand it clearly and before there has been ample guided practice in the classroom. Much of the frustration with homework assignments comes from the fact that students are asked to work independently with material before they are ready. (p. 81)

On returning to the classroom, the teacher should take the time to check the student's homework. If the product indicates that the skill or performance has not yet been attained, further instruction is necessary.

The final section of the literacy lesson plan is **suggested reading and/or notes**. Here, resources are cited and space is provided for written comments and lesson modifications. Meeting the unique strengths and needs of each learner is critical. Feel free to adapt each lesson accordingly.

In summary, each literacy lesson plan contains eight sections: (1) domain and area of instruction, (2) intended learning outcome, (3) materials, (4) prereading activity, (5) reading activity, (6) postreading activity, (7) independent practice, and (8) suggested reading and/or notes. Now is a good time to review Figure 2-1.

The answer to the question "What literacy lesson will be devised and taught for Crystal?" is illustrated in the following literacy lesson plan.

## LITERACY LESSON PLAN

## Domain and Area of Instruction

Comprehension and strategic reading for narrative text: Context clues
Literacy stage: Transitional

### Intended Learning Outcome

After reading both silently and aloud a passage from *Walk Two Moons*, the student will complete the cloze passage by verbally supplying the missing words with 90 percent accuracy.

### Materials

- *Walk Two Moons* (Creech, 1994)
- Two copies of the reading passage
- Writing instruments
- Cloze passage based on the reading passage
- Art paper
- Colored pencils

## Prereading Activity

Without showing the book to the student, read aloud the book title, *Walk Two Moons*. Ask her to draw a book jacket based only on the title. After completing the drawing, compare book covers. Discuss similarities and differences.

## Reading Activity

Choose a passage from *Walk Two Moons*. Make two copies. Give the student one copy and have her read it aloud. Follow along with your copy and note any decoding miscues with check marks.

When the student is finished, point out sentences that have miscues. Inquire if they "make sense." Encourage her to correct the miscues by reading the text surrounding them.

## Postreading Activity

Using the previously read passage, prepare a cloze passage. Delete a total of 10 words, choosing from those that were read incorrectly. List the deleted words on a separate sheet of paper. Referring to the list, direct the student to read aloud the cloze passage and verbally supply the missing words.

## Independent Practice

Using a book of her choice, the student will read aloud to a family member or friend for 15 minutes per day.

## Suggested Reading

Creech, S. (1994). *Walk two moons*. New York: Harper Trophy.

## Notes

Part Two: The Literacy Lesson Plans presents 100 detailed plans, 25 per domain. In many, specific books are cited or recommended for use. As adaptability is a characteristic of the plans, substituting books based on the interests and abilities of the reader is recommended. The 101st lesson plan is located in Appendix A: Literacy Lesson Plan Template. I encourage you to use this to devise literacy lessons of your own.

*Part Two*
# The Literacy Lesson Plans

Knowledge is the property of him who can use it. Knowledge creates interest. With skillful teaching, your students will show more and more interest with increasing knowledge of the subject. Never forget the motivational effects of knowledge.

—Joseph Kennedy

CHAPTER *3*

# ○ *Oral and Written Language Lesson Plans*

## Domain and Area of Instruction

○ral and written language: Picture clues
Literacy stage: Initial reading

### Intended Learning Outcome

The student will orally define three to five words from a picture book with 100 percent accuracy.

### Materials

- Picture book
- Worksheet with words to define
- Tape recorder and blank audiocassette

### Prereading Activity

Choose a picture book that depends primarily on the illustrations to portray a minimal story line, such as *Swim, Number Nine Duckling* (Akass, 1995). Introduce the picture book to the student by asking, "What do you think this book is about just by looking at some of the pictures?" Next, discuss how picture clues suggest certain words that might occur in the story. A picture of two children grooming a pony hints at words both similar and different than those suggested by a picture of the same children grooming a dog. So, when the reader encounters an unknown word, a good tip is to look at the picture on the page and think of related words.

## Reading Activity

Assign the student to silently read several pages of the picture book.

## Postreading Activity

Discuss the story with the student. Ask her to define aloud three to five words based on the provided pictures. Prompt her to think about the use of the word in the sentence and the related picture.

## Independent Practice

The student will read the remainder of the picture book at home. Given a worksheet with words based on pictures in the book, she will define each word by recording the definitions with a tape recorder and blank audiocassette. On returning to school, she will play the tape for evaluation of the definitions.

## Suggested Reading

Akass, S. (1995). *Swim, number nine duckling.* Honesdale, PA: Boyds Mills.
Carle, E. (1969). *The very hungry caterpillar.* New York: Philomel.
de Paola, T. (Reteller). (1988). *The legend of the Indian paintbrush.* New York: Putnam.
Sendak, M. (1963). *Where the wild things are.* New York: Harper.

## Notes

# Domain and Area of Instruction

**O**ral and written language: Commas and periods
Literacy stage: Initial reading

### Intended Learning Outcome

The student will punctuate 10 sentences from a self-selected fiction or non-fiction book by adding commas or periods with 80 percent accuracy.

### Materials

- One student-selected fiction or nonfiction book
- Punctuation worksheet
- Writing instruments

### Prereading Activity

Assign the student to visit the library and select a fiction or nonfiction book. The book should be at his independent level, meaning he can read the book without assistance. In unison, read the story aloud. Read slightly ahead of the student, model fluent and expressive reading, and emphasize commas and periods by pausing and stopping fairly dramatically.

### Reading Activity

Each week ask the student to reread aloud a passage from the book that contains approximately 100 words. Listen for proper pausing and stopping at commas and periods and provide relevant comments and corrections.

### Postreading Activity

Prepare a worksheet containing 10 sentences from the book that are not punctuated. Assign the student to silently read the sentences and insert the required commas and periods. Evaluate the worksheet with the student.

### Independent Practice

The student will read the self-selected book to family members or a friend. He will demonstrate how to pause at commas and stop at periods.

**Notes**

_____

_____

_____

_____

_____

_____

## Domain and Area of Instruction

**O**ral and written language: Proofreading
Literacy stage: Initial reading

### Intended Learning Outcome

The student will proofread her handwritten story and correct any errors in letter formation and direction to the teacher's satisfaction.

### Materials

- Daily newspaper
- Paper and writing instruments

### Prewriting Activity

With the student, survey a newspaper advertisement for a local toy store. Direct her to list three items she would like to buy.

Together, take a trip to the store. Locate the three toys and look at each label, identifying similar letters and noting the different styles of writing. Point out that although the letter styles vary, the direction and general form are similar.

### Writing Activity

Assign the student to write a short story about her trip to the toy store. Require her to include the names of the toys she identified, as well as at least five additional details.

## Postwriting Activity

Ask the student to reread her story. Together, review the essay and focus on the letter formation and direction. Discuss and critique the handwriting. Emphasize the necessity of forming letters the correct way and the importance of good handwriting so that others can read and understand the message. If necessary, assign the student to rewrite a final copy.

## Independent Practice

Using the newspaper advertisement as a guide, the student will write a toy wish list. She will reread her list and edit, if necessary, using her best penmanship. Finally, she will give the ad to her parents.

## Notes

# Domain and Area of Instruction

Oral and written language: List writing
Literacy stage: Initial reading

## Intended Learning Outcome

Under supervision, the student will write a five-item shopping list, go to the store, and purchase the items with 100 percent accuracy.

## Materials

- Shopping list (provided by parent)
- $20 (provided by parent)
- Paper and writing instruments

### Prewriting Activity

Arrange and take a field trip to a local supermarket. Here, explore how the store operates, from unloading the trucks to stocking the shelves to operating the cash registers.

### Writing Activity

Obtain a five-item grocery list from the student's parent. Read the list aloud and direct him to write the five items in list form.

### Postwriting Activity

Return with the student to the local supermarket. Ask him to bring the five-item shopping list and $20. Under supervision, have him find the five items, cross off each as he places it in the shopping cart, and proceed to the checkout line. Here, purchase the items.

### Independent Practice

Reinforcing the previous activity, the student will assist his parent in writing the family's weekly shopping list. Next they will go to the store and, under the supervision of the parent, the student will do the shopping.

### Notes

# Domain and Area of Instruction

Oral and written language: Content-specific vocabulary
Literacy stage: Initial reading

## Intended Learning Outcome

Given a list of five words related to cooking utensils and ingredients, the student will pronounce and define them with 90 percent accuracy.

## Materials

- Cookbook with easy-to-read recipes
- Relevant cooking utensils and ingredients
- Worksheet with list of five cooking-related terms
- Paper and writing instruments

## Prereading Activity

Guide the student through a cookbook and demonstrate how to find recipes by using the table of contents. Give her three recipes to locate. Direct her to find the recipes, read them either aloud or silently, and then retell what the recipe makes.

Have the student choose one recipe to "prepare." In the classroom play kitchen, instruct her to read the instructions and assemble the utensils and ingredients, one by one. If necessary, help the student identify and pronounce any unfamiliar words.

## Reading Activity

Give the student a written list of five cooking utensils and ingredients that she used in her recipe. Ask her to pronounce and define these words.

## Postreading Activity

Ask the student to write a short story describing her cooking adventure. Using the story, have her summarize the experience to her classmates.

## Independent Practice

Under the supervision of a parent, the student will choose a second recipe and prepare it at home (brownie mix works well). She will bring the treat to class to share.

### Suggested Reading

Blain, D. (1991). *Boxcar children cookbook.* Morton Grove, IL: Whitman.

Katzen, M., & Henderson, A. (1994). *Pretend soup and other real recipes: A cookbook for preschoolers and up.* Berkeley, CA: Tricycle.

Priceman, M. (1994). *How to make an apple pie and see the world.* New York: Knopf.

### Notes

_____

_____

_____

_____

_____

_____

## Domain and Area of Instruction

Oral and written language: Story writing

Literacy stage: Initial reading

### Intended Learning Outcome

Using a computer and a word-processing program, the student will write the opening sentence or paragraph to a wordless picture book and share it with the class to the teacher's satisfaction.

### Materials

- Books with interesting leads
- Wordless picture books
- Paper and writing instruments
- Computer with word-processing program

### Prewriting Activity

Discuss that young writers learn about writing by reading widely and examining their literature closely. Next, review leads (the opening sentence or paragraph in a piece of writing) by reading several aloud. Ask the student to select a wordless picture book and survey it.

## Writing Activity

Assign the student to write the lead to the wordless picture book. Allow 10–15 minutes for writing. After he has handwritten the first draft, direct him to revise and edit it. After the draft is edited, instruct him to transcribe the handwritten copy by using a computer and a word-processing program.

## Postwriting Activity

Invite the student to read aloud his word-processed lead to the class. Also encourage him to share the wordless picture book with the class.

## Independent Practice

The student will take the wordless picture book home and continue to develop the plot by writing. He will "read" his wordless picture book to a family member or friend.

## Suggested Reading

Recommended books with interesting leads:

Henkes, K. (1991). *Chrysanthemum.* New York: Greenwillow.
Martin, B., Jr. (1964, 1992). *Brown bear, brown bear, what do you see?* New York: Holt.
Ness, E. (1966). *Sam, Bangs, and moonshine.* New York: Holt.

Recommended wordless picture books:

de Paola, T. (1978). *Pancakes for breakfast.* San Diego: Harcourt.
Hoban, T. (1995). *Colors everywhere.* New York: Greenwillow.
Ormerod, J. (1981). *Moonlight.* New York: Lothrop.

## Notes

## Domain and Area of Instruction

Oral and written language: Spelling
Literacy stage: Initial reading

### Intended Learning Outcome

In writing, the student will spell 10 words from the Tic-Tac-Vowel game with 80 percent accuracy. Next, she will state whether the vowel in each word is long or short with 100 percent accuracy.

### Materials

- Note cards, each with a word with a long or short vowel sound
- Tic-Tac-Vowel games
- Paper and writing instruments
- A selection of children's literature

### Prereading Activity

Present to the student 20 note cards, each containing a word with either a long or short vowel sound. Model making two stacks of note cards: words with long vowel sounds and words with short vowel sounds. Shuffle the note cards and ask the student to form the two stacks.

### Reading Activity

Group students into pairs. Give one student in each pair *X* cards and the other student *O* cards. On the opposite side of each card are words containing either long or short vowel sounds. Direct the student with the *X* cards to turn over one card and pronounce the word. If she correctly pronounces it, she places her *X* card on a space of the Tic-Tac-Vowel playing board. Next, have the student with the *O* cards turn over one of her cards and pronounce the word. If correct, she places her *O* card on a space of the Tic-Tac-Vowel playing board. The first player to get Tic-Tac-Vowel wins the game.

After the game is over, administer a spelling-vowel quiz. Choose 10 words from the Tic-Tac-Vowel game. Ask the students to write the pronounced words. Next, have them spell each word aloud and identify the vowel sound as either long or short.

### Postreading Activity

Ask the student to select a book to survey. Instruct her to find 10 words that she can read and then list them in writing. Have her pronounce each word and identify the vowels as long or short.

### Independent Practice

The student will take the Tic-Tac-Vowel game home to play with family members or friends. On returning to school, she will report who won the game.

### Notes

_____

_____

_____

_____

_____

## Domain and Area of Instruction

**O**ral and written language: Fluency
Literacy stage: Initial reading

### Intended Learning Outcome

The student and three classmates will select a picture book that contains several characters who dialogue frequently. Choosing roles, they will read their lines, rehearse, and perform a Readers Theatre (Sloyer, 1982). They will present their narrative piece to students in another class, using proper intonation, inflection, and fluency to the teacher's satisfaction.

### Materials

- Picture book suitable for Readers Theatre
- Highlighted scripts
- Paper and writing instruments

### Prereading Activity

Instruct the students to attend story time at the public library. Have them observe and take notes on what story was read and why they enjoyed listening.

Assign them to also interview the story reader. With guidance from the story reader or teacher, ask the students to choose a book from which to perform a Readers Theatre.

Readers Theatre provides a realistic opportunity for students to read orally and practice intonation, inflection, and fluency. A narrative story or passage is selected, character parts are assigned, and appropriate sections for oral reading are identified and practiced. Following rehearsal, the students read their scripts orally for an audience. Props and costumes are not necessary.

## Reading Activity

Using the selected book, create highlighted scripts that make clear each actor's respective lines. Read the story and rehearse the presentation. Also assign the actors to generate at least three questions to ask a prospective audience.

## Postreading Activity

Arrange with a colleague to present the production to his class, preferably a class with younger students. When the actors finish, have them ask the audience their questions. Promote discussion.

## Independent Practice

The actors will compose and write a thank-you note to the audience. Suggest that they include why they enjoyed performing, and encourage them to include drawings.

## Suggested Reading

Alborough, J. (1997). *Watch out! Big Bro's coming!* Cambridge, MA: Candlewick Press.

Archambault, J., & Martin, B. Jr. (1994). *A beautiful feast for a big king cat.* New York: HarperCollins.

Sloyer, S. (1982). *Readers theatre: Story dramatization in the classroom.* Urbana, IL: National Council of Teachers of English.

Waddell, M. (1992). *Owl babies.* New York: Candlewick Press.

## Notes

_____

_____

_____

_____

_____

_____

_____

## Domain and Area of Instruction

Oral and written language: Word meanings
Literacy stage: Transitional

### Intended Learning Outcome

The student will write an original selection containing 10 previously unknown words. The words will be spelled correctly and used in appropriate context with 80 percent accuracy.

### Materials

- Self-selected trade book
- Paper and writing instruments
- Dictionary

### Prereading Activity

Ask the student to select a book in which she is interested and which contains or is likely to contain new vocabulary. Explain how context clues such as picture clues, expectancy clues, and meaning clues help identify and define unknown words. Picture clues suggest certain sets of words that might occur in the story; expectancy clues are based on what is already known about the topic; meaning clues use words surrounding an unknown word to define it.

### Reading Activity

Assign the student to read the selected book. As she encounters unknown words, direct her to add them to a list until there is a total of 10. Tell her to use context clues to write her best guess for the meaning of each word. Then, have her consult a dictionary, copy the correct definition, and make a comparison.

### Postreading Activity

Instruct the student to compose a story, poem, or report that contains the 10 new words. Allow time for revising, proofreading, and editing. With the student, evaluate her best draft for spelling and accuracy of word usage.

### Independent Practice

The student will make a conscious effort to use one or more of the 10 words in speaking or writing on a daily basis. She will report on her progress and the manner in which she used the words in context.

### Notes

_____

_____

_____

_____

_____

## Domain and Area of Instruction

Oral and written language: Fluency
Literacy stage: Transitional

### Intended Learning Outcome

Given the first chapter of *Me and the Man on the Moon-eyed Horse*, the student will read it aloud to a class of second-graders, demonstrating proper use of enunciation, expression, and volume to the teacher's satisfaction.

## Materials

- *Me and the Man on the Moon-eyed Horse* (Fleischman, 1977)
- Tape recorder and blank audiocassette
- Pioneer costume

## Prereading Activity

Dressed in a pioneer costume, dramatically read aloud the first chapter of *Me and the Man on the Moon-eyed Horse*. Introduce the concept of fluency and its related characteristics: enunciation, expression, and volume. Explain that enunciation is clarity of speech, expression conveys emotion, and volume is the loudness of sound.

## Reading Activity

Using echo reading (Walker, 1992), read aloud with the student the first chapter of *Me and the Man on the Moon-eyed Horse*. In echo reading, the teacher fluently reads one sentence of text aloud. The student then attempts to imitate the oral reading model. The reading continues in this manner until the student can independently read the text with fluency.

Next, instruct the student to read the chapter into a tape recorder and then to rewind the tape. Have him listen to the recording and self-critique it for proper use of enunciation, expression, and volume.

## Postreading Activity

Arrange for the student to visit another class, preferably at a lower grade level. Instruct him to read aloud the first chapter of the book, focusing on fluency and its attributes.

## Independent Practice

The student will practice reading aloud the second chapter of *Me and the Man on the Moon-eyed Horse*. He will make arrangements with the participating teacher to continue to be a guest reader until the book is completed.

## Suggested Reading

Fleischman, S. (1977). *Me and the man on the moon-eyed horse*. Boston: Little, Brown.

Walker, B. J. (1992). *Diagnostic teaching of reading: Techniques for instruction and assessment*. New York: Macmillan.

## Notes

_____

_____

_____

_____

_____

## Domain and Area of Instruction

Oral and written language: Punctuation (quotation marks)
Literacy stage: Transitional

### Intended Learning Outcome

Using dialogue paragraphs lacking quotation marks, the student will fill in the quotation marks with 80 percent accuracy.

### Materials

- Cartoon worksheets
- Worksheet with dialogue paragraphs lacking quotation marks
- Paper and writing instruments

### Prewriting Activity

Request the student to dictate a conversation. Transcribe the story, modeling how to place proper punctuation where necessary. Together, examine the story and focus on the quotations.

Give the student a cartoon worksheet explaining that when words "fall out of someone's mouth," they land in quotation marks. The worksheet should include blank cartoons so that the student can fill in her own words, reinforcing the idea that dialogue is surrounded by quotation marks.

### Writing Activity

Give the student a worksheet with dialogue statements lacking quotation marks. Read the statements and request her to place quotation marks in the appropriate places. After she completes the worksheet, assign her to write a short story that includes conversation between two people. Remind her to use quotation marks when words fall out of the speaker's mouths.

## Postwriting Activity

Using a worksheet containing 10 additional dialogues lacking required quotation marks, assign the student to write the quotation marks in the appropriate places. On completion, evaluate the worksheet and prompt her to explain why she supplied the punctuation.

## Independent Practice

Outside of the classroom, the student will write an adventure story with a minimum of two characters. She will supply quotation marks when necessary. On returning to the classroom, the story will be critiqued by either classmates or the teacher.

## Notes

_____

_____

_____

_____

_____

# Domain and Area of Instruction

Oral and written language: Aesthetic listening
Literacy stage: Transitional

## Intended Learning Outcome

After listening to the tape-recorded version of *Jumanji*, the student will draw two mental images on separate sheets of paper and write under each a brief, descriptive summary, demonstrating his comprehension of the story to the teacher's satisfaction.

## Materials

- Tape-recorded version of *Jumanji* (Van Allsburg, 1981) as recorded by Williams (1995)
- Sign language interpreter
- Tape player
- Paper, writing instruments, and drawing materials

## Prereading Activity

Arrange and invite a sign language interpreter to visit the class. Ask the students to name foreign languages; record the list on the board. If no student mentions American Sign Language (ASL), ask if anyone knows the name of the language used by many deaf Americans, and, if necessary, supply the answer.

Introduce the guest speaker. Inquire if anyone knows any ASL signs and provide time for demonstrations. Next, have the sign language interpreter introduce the ASL signs for *game, lion, monkey, rain,* and *snake.* Finally, ask the class to predict persons, places, or things in the story *Jumanji.*

## Reading Activity

Explain to the class that they will be listening to the tape-recorded version of *Jumanji* and practicing mental imagery. Define mental imagery as "drawing a picture in one's mind" and emphasize that mental imagery enhances under-standing or comprehension.

With the students, design a chart listing the mental imagery steps: close your eyes, draw a picture in your mind of what you hear, and add details and colors to the mental image. Next, play the tape and stop after a few sentences to describe the image formed in your mind. Continue to play the tape and stop periodically for students to describe their mental images.

## Postreading Activity

After listening to the story, assign the students to draw two of their mental images on separate sheets of paper. Ask them to also write brief descriptive summaries under each drawing.

Have the students share their drawings and arrange them according to the sequence of the story. Display the artwork in the classroom.

## Independent Practice

The student will retell the story line of *Jumanji* to a friend or family member. He will explain what a mental image is and ask the listener to form one. On returning to the classroom, he will report what happened.

### Suggested Reading

Van Allsburg, C. (1981). *Jumanji*. Boston: Houghton Mifflin.

Williams, R. (Reader). (1995). *Jumanji* [Cassette Recording]. Boston: Houghton Mifflin.

### Notes

_____

_____

_____

_____

_____

## Domain and Area of Instruction

Oral and written language: Structured writing activities

Literacy stage: Transitional

### Intended Learning Outcome

After listening to and discussing sections of the book *If You Were a Writer*, the student will respond to a statement by writing at least four sentences in her reading response journal.

### Materials

- Assortment of objects on a table
- Number tags
- Paper and writing instruments
- *If You Were a Writer* (Nixon, 1988)
- Newsprint
- Markers
- Reader response journals
- Board and chalk

## Prereading Activity

Arrange on a small table at the front of the classroom a number of objects: a tape measure, a calculator, a stethoscope, a map and compass, a needle and thread, a bowl and a wire whisk, a palette and paintbrush, and a typewriter. Attach a number to each object or set, ranging from 1 to 8. Display the items all morning so the students can observe them.

Ask the students to guess what occupation each of the items or sets represents by writing the number and its occupation on a sheet of paper. Elicit answers by asking the questions "What is this?" and "Who would use this object?" Save the typewriter for last, because this item introduces the reading activity.

## Reading Activity

Read sections of the book *If You Were a Writer* aloud and tell the students to listen for specific clues about what writers do. Next, ask, "After listening to the story, what are a writer's most important tools?" As the students respond, list their comments on a large piece of newsprint.

## Postreading Activity

Direct the students to their work places with their writing instruments and reading response journals. A reader response journal is a type of journal in which the student records her ideas and feelings about what she has read.

Write the following on the board: *Describe your best friend. Write at least four sentences, and use words that create a clear picture in the reader's mind.* Allow 15 minutes for writing.

Collect and read silently the journal entries. Write at least one positive comment and one question in each student's journal. Return the journals to the writers.

## Independent Practice

The student will read the comments and question and answer the teacher's query in her reader response journal.

## Suggested Reading

Nixon, J. L. (1988). *If you were a writer.* New York: Simon & Schuster.

**Notes**

## Domain and Area of Instruction

**O**ral and written language: Poetry
Literacy stage: Transitional

### Intended Learning Outcome

The student with a partner will create and perform a dual narrative poem with 75 percent accuracy as determined by the following criteria: equal voice, transitions between speaking, creativity, and collaboration.

### Materials

- Copies of a selection from *Joyful Noise: Poems for Two Voices* (Fleischman, 1988)
- Paper and writing instruments
- Poetry evaluation form

### Prereading Activity

Perform with another person a selection from *Joyful Noise: Poems for Two Voices*. Discuss how the oral readers must pronounce and articulate the poet's language appropriately. The reader's tonal qualities, timing, and intonation levels influence the listener's interpretation of the poem.

### Reading Activity

Pair students and have them reread the poem. Instruct them to create their own poems based on the demonstration. Explain that the activity will be evaluated on the following criteria: equal voice, transitions between speaking, creativity, and collaboration. Require each team to submit a final copy of their poem. Allow adequate time for composing and rehearsing.

## Postreading Activity

In pairs, have the students perform their poems. Evaluate each performance by completing a poetry evaluation form and discussing it with the duo. Compile a class poetry book or display the poems.

## Independent Practice

The student will take home a copy of his poem. He will find a partner to rehearse and read aloud the piece.

## Suggested Reading

Fleischman, P. (1986). *I am Phoenix: Poems for two voices.* New York: Harper.
Fleischman, P. (1988). *Joyful noise: Poems for two voices.* New York: Harper.
Olaleye, I. (1995). *The distant talking drum.* Honesdale, PA: Boyds Mills/
    Wordsong.
Thayer, E. (1888, 1989). *Casey at the bat.* New York: Putnam.

## Notes

## Domain and Area of Instruction

**O**ral and written language: Comprehension
Literacy stage: Transitional

### Intended Learning Outcome

Given a teacher-made written cloze selection based on the selected book, the student will fill in the blanks with 50 percent accuracy.

### Materials

- Book with predictable patterns
- Teacher-made oral cloze selection
- Teacher-made written cloze selection
- Writing instruments

### Prereading Activity

Read aloud a passage with a predictable pattern, emphasizing the predictable parts by using an enthusiastic voice. Reread the passage and ask the student to join in when she knows what to say.

Describe the cloze procedure. This requires the reader to fill in blanks for words that have been systematically deleted from a selected passage. Demonstrate an oral cloze procedure in which every 10th word in a 200-word passage is deleted. Next, allow the student to rehearse by orally providing the missing words.

### Reading Activity

Assign the student to read the remainder of the book silently.

### Postreading Activity

Using a passage from the book, assign the student to complete a written cloze selection. Evaluate and share the results with the student.

To construct the cloze selection, select a passage containing about 250 to 300 words. Leave the first sentence intact. Beginning with the second sentence, delete words at a consistent interval, for example, every 10th word, for a total of 50 deletions. Replace the deleted words with blanks of equal length. Duplicate the desired number of copies. Regarding scoring, only one word goes in each blank, misspellings are not counted as errors, and only exact words are acceptable as correct responses (Bormuth, 1975).

### Independent Practice

The student will reread the book to someone outside the classroom. She will retell how predictable language promotes comprehension.

### Suggested Reading

Bormuth, J. R. (1975). The cloze procedure: Literacy in the classroom. In W. D. Page (Ed.), *Help for the reading teacher: New directions in research* (pp. 60–90). Urbana, IL: ERIC Clearinghouse on Reading and Communication Skills.

Galdone, P. (1971). *Three Aesop fox fables.* New York: Clarion.

Guarino, D. (1989). *Is your mama a llama?* New York: Scholastic.

Marzollo, J. (1990). *Pretend you're a cat.* New York: Dial.

### Notes

_____

_____

_____

_____

_____

_____

## Domain and Area of Instruction

**O**ral and written language: Writing friendly letters
Literacy stage: Transitional

### Intended Learning Outcome

Using the standard five parts of a friendly letter (the heading, the salutation, the body, the closing, and the signature), the student will write a friendly letter that includes three complete ideas in the body of the letter.

### Materials

- Model of a friendly letter
- Paper and writing instruments

## Prewriting Activity

Discuss the standard format for writing a friendly letter. Show an example of a letter that includes a heading, salutation, body, closing, and signature, all labeled clearly. Collaboratively with the student, write a short letter. Prior to writing the body of the letter, elicit orally from the student ideas that could be included. Record the ideas. Next, assign him to write the body, choosing three of the brainstormed ideas. When the assignment is completed, ask him to identify the five parts of a friendly letter.

## Writing Activity

Assign the student to write a friendly letter to anyone he chooses. Prior to writing the body, suggest that he brainstorm ideas, jot them down, and then choose three or more to create the body.

## Postwriting Activity

As a team, proofread the letter. Have the student revise and edit accordingly.

## Independent Practice

The student will choose a friend or relative to whom he will write on a regular basis. By doing so, he will reinforce and practice the skill of letter writing.

## Notes

# Domain and Area of Instruction

Oral and written language: Stretching the sentence
Literacy stage: Basic literacy

## Intended Learning Outcome

Using original sentences from a creative writing piece, the student will write five stretched sentences with 80 percent accuracy.

## Materials

- Paper and writing instruments
- An original writing piece
- Board and chalk

## Prewriting Activity

Read aloud a simple sentence and write it on the board, for example, *The dog ran*. Ask a student to identify the action. If the response is *run* or *running*, continue probing until the specific verb is named. Double-underline the verb.

Next, ask who or what ran? When the student answers, underline the word *dog*. Explain that more words can be added to the sentence to provide more description; for example, *The brown dog ran down the street*. Announce that this strategy is called stretching the sentence.

## Writing Activity

Using a former creative writing piece, assign the student to stretch five of the original sentences. When she has completed the assignment, have her edit and write a final copy.

## Postwriting Activity

Ask the student to write samples of the original and the stretched sentences on the board. Discuss and critique with her classmates.

## Independent Practice

The student will compose a creative story. When it is completed, she will apply sentence stretching to several sentences. Next, she will read the piece to a family member or friend and, finally, explain the process of stretching the sentence.

**Notes**

_____

_____

_____

_____

_____

_____

## Domain and Area of Instruction

Oral and written language: Idea development
Literacy stage: Basic literacy

### Intended Learning Outcome

After direct instruction in semantic mapping, the student will draw a semantic map for a story theme that contains at least five details.

### Materials

- Paper and writing instruments
- Board and chalk

### Prewriting Activity

Demonstrate how to create a semantic map to organize thoughts, develop ideas, and create a well-developed story.

A semantic map (Freedman & Reynolds, 1980) is a visual display of the relationships in the composition of a story or expository selection. First, the core question or theme of the story is written in the center. Next, the answers or related ideas branch from the center core to form strands. Finally, specific facts, events, and ideas relevant to each strand are connected to that strand (see Figure 3-1).

### Writing Activity

Arrange the students into groups based on interests. This provides choice and encourages them to accept responsibility for their own learning. Assign one

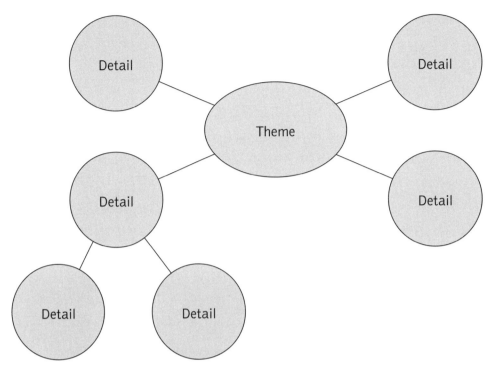

**Figure 3-1.**   Semantic map protocol.

student in each group to write the first sentence to a creative story. Passing the sentences counterclockwise, instruct each of the remaining group members to add a word to the original sentence, thus expanding the ideas of the preceding authors. When they are finished, ask one student in each group to write on the board both the original sentence and the final developed sentence. Compare sentences and discuss.

### Postwriting Activity

Based on their expanded sentences, assign each group to design a semantic map. The semantic map must have at least five details that relate to the main idea.

### Independent Practice

Using the expanded sentence and the semantic map, each student will independently write a creative story. On returning to the classroom, the student will read his composition aloud and compare it to others.

### Suggested Reading

Freedman, G., & Reynolds, E. G. (1980). Enriching basal reader lessons with semantic webbing. *The Reading Teacher, 34,* 677–684.

**Notes**

_____

_____

_____

_____

_____

_____

## Domain and Area of Instruction

**O**ral and written language: Note taking
Literacy stage: Basic literacy

### Intended Learning Outcome

After silently reading and taking notes from a passage in the social studies text-book, the student, using her notes, will complete a 10-question worksheet with 90 percent accuracy.

### Materials

- Social studies textbook
- Videotaping equipment
- Social studies worksheet
- Paper and writing instruments

### Prereading Activity

Give a five-minute lecture about the social studies topic. Arrange to have someone videotape it. Instruct the students to listen without taking notes. After listening to the lecture, give the students an oral quiz based on the main ideas and supporting details. Orally correct the quiz.

Next, view the videotape of the lecture and instruct the students to take notes on the information presented. Administer a similar quiz. Encourage the students to use their notes. Compare scores from the first quiz to those of the second. Emphasize that notes serve as a successful warehouse for lecture information; then, model several strategies for taking notes.

Note-taking strategies include outlining, summarizing paragraphs, and drawing main points and supporting details. Because many procedures exist, consult content area reading and study skills texts, such as *Content Area Reading: Literacy and Learning across the Curriculum* (Vacca & Vacca, 1999) and *The College Learner: Reading, Studying, and Attaining Academic Success* (Jalongo, Twiest, & Gerlach, 1999) for specifics.

## Reading Activity

Organize students into groups of three. Using a chapter from the social studies textbook, assign each group to read one of three sections and to take notes on the information presented. From their collective notes, have each group summarize the information gleaned. Make copies of each group's notes and distribute them to each member of the class.

## Postreading Activity

Assign the students to complete a 10-question worksheet based on the main ideas and details of the chapter. Encourage them to use their notes. Orally provide the answers as the students grade their own worksheets. Discuss.

## Independent Practice

At home, the student will read and take notes on a newspaper article that is at least 15 paragraphs long. On returning to class and using her notes, she will summarize the main ideas and supporting details of the article.

## Suggested Reading

Jalongo, M., Twiest, M. M., & Gerlach, G. (1999). *The college learner: Reading, studying, and attaining academic success* (2nd ed.). Columbus, OH: Merrill/ Prentice Hall.

Vacca, R. T., & Vacca, J. L. (1999). *Content area reading: Literacy and learning across the curriculum* (6th ed.). New York: Longman.

## Notes

## Domain and Area of Instruction

ral and written language: Writing multiple cohesive paragraphs
Literacy stage: Basic literacy

### Intended Learning Outcome

Given a semantic map that randomly displays multiple facts about a chosen topic, the student will group the facts into categories and then write a paragraph for each of the categories. Each paragraph will have a topic sentence and several supporting sentences.

### Materials

- Short video about chosen topic
- Short article or books about chosen topic
- Board and chalk
- Handouts of the Analytic Scoring System for Writing (adapted from Gipe, 1998)
- Paper and writing instruments

### Prewriting Activity

View a short video about the chosen topic, for example, volcanoes. Next, collaboratively create a semantic map about the topic. The word *volcano* will be in the center of the map. As the students think of varied ideas related to the topic, merely branch the supporting details out from the center word, *volcano*, in random order.

### Writing Activity

Assign each student to organize the random ideas on the semantic map into logical categories. Some of the ideas may not fit into a category; it is not necessary to use every idea. Next, instruct them to write a topic sentence for each category of ideas and then to expand each paragraph by writing several supporting sentences.

## Postwriting Activity

Direct the students to exchange essays. Using the Analytic Scoring System for Writing handout, have each student assess the quality of the essay by examining the areas of ideas, organization, style, and mechanics (see Figure 3-2). Provide time for each evaluator to share his findings with the writer. Instruct the writer to edit accordingly.

## Independent Practice

The student will read a short story or book about the chosen topic. Based on the story, he will create a semantic map and then write at least two paragraphs. Each paragraph must have a topic sentence and several supporting sentences. On returning to the classroom, he will read his essay aloud for everyone's enjoyment.

## Suggested Reading

Gipe, J. P. (1998). *Multiple paths to literacy: Corrective techniques for classroom teachers* (4th ed.). Upper Saddle River, NJ: Prentice-Hall.

## Notes

_____

_____

_____

_____

_____

_____

_____

Name _____

|  | Strong 3 | Average 2 | Weak 1 |
|---|---|---|---|

**Ideas**
1. Ideas are creative.                      ____   ____   ____
2. Ideas are well developed.                ____   ____   ____
3. Audience and purpose are considered.     ____   ____   ____
*Average ideas  =*                                          ____

**Organization**
1. An organizational pattern is used.       ____   ____   ____
2. Ideas are presented in logical order.    ____   ____   ____
3. Topic sentences are clear.               ____   ____   ____
*Average organization  =*                                   ____

**Style**
1. A good choice of words is displayed.     ____   ____   ____
2. Figurative language is used.             ____   ____   ____
3. A variety of sentence patterns is used.  ____   ____   ____
*Average style  =*                                          ____

**Mechanics**
1. Most words are spelled correctly.        ____   ____   ____
2. Punctuation and capitalization
   are used correctly.                      ____   ____   ____
3. Standard language is used.               ____   ____   ____

*Average mechanics  =*                                      ____

*Average paper  =*                                          ____

Comments

_____

_____

_____

_____

**Figure 3-2.**    The Analytic Scoring System for Writing.

*Source:* Adapted with permission from *Multiple Paths to Literacy 4/e* by Joan P. Gipe. Copyright © 1998. Reprinted by permission of Prentice-Hall, Inc., Upper Saddle River, N.J.

## Domain and Area of Instruction

Oral and written language: Writing development
Literacy stage: Basic literacy

### Intended Learning Outcome

The student will write 10 journal entries in her reader response journal about her feelings and reactions to the book *The Giver*.

### Materials

- *The Giver* (Lowry, 1993)
- Reader response journal
- Writing instruments

### Prewriting Activity

Introduce *The Giver* to the student. Together, read the first few pages. Next, ask, "What is the theme of the book?" Share your initial reactions to the story.

### Writing Activity

Assign Chapters 1 and 2 as silent reading. When she is finished, instruct her to write at least two pages in her reader response journal, describing her reactions to the book. Reinforce focusing on content rather than punctuation and grammar.

### Postwriting Activity

Over a two-week period, direct the student to continue to read the book, reflect on it, and write in her journal. Periodically, collect the journal, read it, and write positive responses. Return the journal promptly for review and reinforcement.

### Independent Practice

Over the two-week period, the student will read and write in her reader response journal. She will also read the written comments. This process promotes reflection and gives the instructor useful insights about the writer.

### Suggested Reading

Lowry, L. (1993). *The giver*. Boston: Houghton Mifflin.

**Notes**

_____

_____

_____

_____

_____

_____

## Domain and Area of Instruction

**O**ral and written language: Note taking
Literacy stage: Basic literacy

### Intended Learning Outcome

After silently reading a passage from a magazine of his choice, the student will take notes and, using his notes, orally summarize the information to the teacher's satisfaction.

### Materials

- Five-minute lecture on tape
- Tape recorder and blank audiocassette
- Magazines
- Paper and writing instruments

### Prereading Activity

Provide instruction on characteristics of good note taking. For example, high-quality notes are legible, use abbreviations, capture main ideas and supporting details, and record information selectively. Next, direct the student to listen to a 5-minute lecture on audiocassette and to take notes. Critique the notes and provide relevant instruction. Finally, verbally quiz the student on main ideas and supporting details, emphasizing the importance of note taking.

### Reading Activity

Provide magazines for the student. Instruct him to choose one and to read one article while taking notes. Reinforce applying the characteristics of good note-taking.

### Postreading Activity

Confer with the student regarding the contents of the notes. Orally quiz him on the main ideas and supporting details of the magazine article, allowing him to refer to his notes.

### Independent Practice

The student will practice note taking. While listening to a commercial, presentation, or directions, he will take notes and summarize the main ideas and supporting details.

### Notes

_____

_____

_____

_____

_____

## Domain and Area of Instruction

Oral and written language: Composing and transcribing
Literacy stage: Basic literacy

### Intended Learning Outcome

To differentiate between composing and transcribing, the student will write daily in a personal journal and then choose five entries to transcribe. Each transcription will be a minimum of one page and will describe a self-selected experience.

## Materials

- Personal journal
- Writing instruments

## Prewriting Activity

Discuss the difference between composing and transcribing. Composing is the ongoing process of generating and shaping ideas before writing and as the actual writing unfolds. Composing involves thinking about ideas, weighing them, and arranging them in some kind of order. Transcribing describes the mechanics of writing—spelling, punctuation, capitalization, format, and neatness. During the early stages of writing, the writer should focus on composing rather than the attributes of transcribing.

Prior to vacation, instruct the student to include in her suitcase a personal journal and writing instruments. To focus on composing, encourage her to write daily in her journal. To focus on transcribing, instruct her to choose five entries and transcribe each into a one-page essay.

## Writing Activity

While on vacation, the student will practice composing by writing daily activities, thoughts, and reflections in her personal journal.

## Postwriting Activity

The student will practice transcribing by choosing five journal entries and transcribing each. The final products will be five one-page essays. On returning to the classroom, the writer will share the compositions with the teacher.

## Independent Practice

The student will independently maintain her personal journal.

## Notes

# Domain and Area of Instruction

**O**ral and written language: Creative writing
Literacy stage: Basic literacy

## Intended Learning Outcome

By providing written responses to 10 of the 14 Assignment Mastery queries, the student will optimally prepare to complete a creative writing assignment.

## Materials

- Assignment Mastery handout (adapted from Strickland, 1975)
- Paper and writing instruments or a computer with a word-processing program

## Prewriting Activity

Introduce the Assignment Mastery handout that contains the following questions:

*Scanning*
- How difficult does the work appear to be?
- Is it a relatively large amount of work?
- Will I have to alter my schedule to get it done?
- Are the terms generally familiar?
- What is the main theme of the assignment?
- What main headings and subheadings are there?
- What specialized vocabulary is stressed?

*Preparation for reading*
- Are there related terms that I use?
- Have I learned something that changes the meaning of the term(s)?
- Does the theme of the material challenge or support my ideas?

*Reading*
- What is the meaning of what I am reading?
- What illustrations of that meaning are given?
- Can I recall any personal examples that clarify the meaning of the material?
- What questions should I ask the instructor to clarify the meaning of this material?

Explain how asking oneself relevant questions provides a personal purpose for completing an assignment.

## Writing Activity

Give the student the following creative writing scenario: You are a time traveler; the setting is the Western Hemisphere prior to 1492. Using your modern-day knowledge, your purpose is to prepare the inhabitants for the arrival of Columbus. You must decide how you will proceed by first constructing an outline stating your purpose, your main idea, your supporting ideas, the sequence of your plan or action, and the probable outcome.

To prepare for the assignment and to enhance comprehension, instruct the student to answer in writing at least 10 of the 14 Assignment Mastery questions.

## Postwriting Activity

Invite the student to share his Assignment Mastery responses. Discuss accordingly and then encourage him to construct the outline.

## Independent Practice

The student will compose the first draft of his outline. On returning to class, peers will read and respond to one another's drafts.

## Suggested Reading

Strickland, E. (1975, October). Assignment mastery. *Reading World*, 25–31.

## Notes

## Domain and Area of Instruction

Oral and written language: Context and synonyms
Literacy stage: Basic literacy

### Intended Learning Outcome

The student will select five unknown words from each chapter of *Yolanda's Genius* and use a thesaurus to provide synonyms for each selected word with 80 percent accuracy per chapter.

### Materials

- *Yolanda's Genius* (Fenner, 1995)
- Blues festival posters
- Tape player
- *Blues Masters* (O'Neal, 1993) audiocassette
- Guest harmonica player
- Board and chalk
- Thesaurus
- Paper and writing instruments

### Prereading Activity

Ask students what they already know about blues music. Using the *Blues Masters* audiocassette, play a sample blues selection. Ask students to identify distinctive sounds and instruments played. Also invite a guest harmonica player to demonstrate a blues tune. Finally, introduce *Yolanda's Genius*, a story about a boy who communicates with his harmonica.

### Reading Activity

Assign the students to read silently the first chapter of the book.

### Postreading Activity

Arrange the students in pairs. Instruct each duo to choose five unknown words from Chapter 1 and write down the page numbers where they are located. Next, ask them to write their five words on the board.

Review each word with the class. Inquire about each meaning and how to decode or figure it out. Then, have each pair read the word in its original sentence. Again, discuss the word's meaning and the benefits of using the words surrounding an unknown target word to trigger recognition or meaning. This is context, a cue system for decoding unknown words.

Using a thesaurus and the five target words, assign each pair to choose a synonym for each. Ask them to write an original story using the new words or the synonyms. Check to see if the sentences make sense.

## Independent Practice

The student will continue to read *Yolanda's Genius*. After reading each chapter, she will choose five unknown words, decode them by using context, select appropriate synonyms, and write an original story using the new terms. Periodically, the instructor will review the student's work.

## Suggested Reading

Fenner, C. (1995). *Yolanda's genius*. New York: Aladdin.

O'Neal, J. (Compiler). (1993). *Blues masters* (Cassette Recording No. R471128). Los Angeles: Rhino.

## Notes

CHAPTER 4
# W Word Recognition Lesson Plans

---

## Domain and Area of Instruction

Word recognition: Phonics
Literacy stage: Initial reading

### Intended Learning Outcome

Given 10 nursery rhyme lines with the initial letter from a key word omitted, the student will fill in the correct letter from a choice of four with 80 percent accuracy.

### Materials

- Selection of nursery rhymes, such as *Counting Rhymes* (McKellar, 1993), or poems
- Worksheet containing 10 nursery rhyme lines, each with one initial letter omitted per line; provide four letter-choice options per line
- Writing instruments

### Prereading Activity

Give the student a list of five commonly used nursery rhyme words. Using the first word, brainstorm and write a list of possible rhyming words, for example, *moon* = *spoon, soon, noon, loony tune, Daniel Boone*. Use the same procedure for the remaining four rhyme words.

### Reading Activity

Assign the student to read silently a nursery rhyme or poem. From these readings, construct a worksheet containing 10 nursery rhyme lines. For each line, delete one initial letter of a key rhyming word. Provide four letter-choice options per omission.

### Postreading Activity

Using the worksheet, direct the student to read each line and fill in the missing letter from the choice of letters provided. Discuss responses.

### Independent Practice

The student will choose a nursery rhyme or poem and read it. Then he will express his personal reaction to it by drawing a picture.

### Suggested Reading

Bemelmans, L. (1939, 1962). *Madeline*. New York: Viking.
Fleming, D. (1994). *Barnyard banter*. New York: Holt.
Martin, B. Jr. (1991). *Polar bear, polar bear, what do you hear?* New York: Holt.
McKellar, S. (1993). *Counting rhymes*. New York: Dorling.

### Notes

## Domain and Area of Instruction

**W**ord recognition: Phonics
Literacy stage: Initial reading

### Intended Learning Outcome

When given 20 pairs of rhyming words, the first with an initial consonant sound and the second with an initial blend or digraph, and the teacher pronounces the first word, the student will pronounce the second word with 80 percent accuracy.

### Materials

- *Fox in Socks* (Geisel, 1987)
- Phonics worksheet
- Writing instruments

### Prereading Activity

Discuss beginning consonant sounds and beginning blends. Give some examples: *rub/scrub, pin/twin*. Using *Fox in Socks*, survey the book with the student and make a list of rhyming words with different beginning sounds. When finished, ask her to read aloud the list.

### Reading Activity

Read aloud to the student *Fox in Socks*.

### Postreading Activity

Given the phonics worksheet (see Figure 4-1), allow the student to preread the 20 pairs of words silently. Next, read aloud the first word in each pair; ask the student to read aloud the second word in each pair.

### Independent Practice

The student will write a short poem or story using at least three pairs of rhyming words with different beginning sounds. On returning to school, she will read her poem or story aloud.

### Suggested Reading

Geisel, T. S. (Dr. Seuss). (1987). *Fox in socks*. New York: Random Library.

| | | | |
|---|---|---|---|
| 1. bell<br>   shell | 6. day<br>   gray | 11. rice<br>    slice | 16. bag<br>    drag |
| 2. mile<br>   while | 7. sing<br>   sting | 12. rain<br>    plain | 17. mother<br>    smother |
| 3. hem<br>   them | 8. lace<br>   space | 13. perk<br>    clerk | 18. head<br>    spread |
| 4. fin<br>   thin | 9. bat<br>   flat | 14. find<br>    blind | 19. peak<br>    sneak |
| 5. seat<br>   cheat | 10. dance<br>    glance | 15. seek<br>    creek | 20. dare<br>    square |

**Figure 4-1.**   Phonics worksheet.

## Notes

_____

_____

_____

_____

_____

# Domain and Area of Instruction

**W**ord recognition: Sight vocabulary
Literacy stage: Initial reading

### Intended Learning Outcome

After a list of 10 letters is projected for one minute, from memory the student will write the letters in order with 80 percent accuracy.

## Materials

- Overhead projector, screen, markers, and transparencies
- Hat
- Words written on slips of paper
- Writing instruments
- Board and chalk

## Prereading Activity

Write a row of numbers on a transparency. Using an overhead projector, reveal them for one minute; then turn off the projector. Ask the student to write the numbers from memory. Check for accuracy by reviewing the transparency. Repeat the activity with longer sequences of numbers.

## Reading Activity

Write words from a current story on pieces of paper and place them in a hat. Ask the student to draw a word and read it aloud. Write the word on the board. Continue until five words are written. Give the student three minutes to study the five words. Then, cover the words and ask him to write them in order on paper. Continue the procedure until a sequence of seven words is listed and written.

## Postreading Activity

Project a list of 10 letters for one minute. Turn off the projector. Ask the student to write the letters in order from memory.

## Independent Practice

Without looking, the student will ask a parent or family member to put several kitchen utensils on a tray and cover them. Then the parent will reveal the utensils for a few seconds and cover the tray, and the student will list in writing as many utensils as he can remember. On returning to school, the list will be shared with the teacher.

## Notes

_____

_____

_____

_____

_____

_____

## Domain and Area of Instruction

**W**ord recognition: Sight vocabulary
Literacy stage: Initial reading

### Intended Learning Outcome

Given a list of 10 sight words chosen from the student's dictated and transcribed story, she will pronounce the words with 90 percent accuracy.

### Materials

- Student's self-selected photo
- Computer and word-processing program
- Printer with paper
- Marker
- Laminated checkerboard
- Checkers
- Student's personal dictionary
- Writing instruments

### Prereading Activity

Ask the student to bring to class her favorite photo. Elicit a description of, or story about, the image. Transcribe her contribution by using a computer and word-processing program. Print two copies of the story.

Using the learner's language and experiences as a base to teach reading is called the language experience approach (LEA). Saving LEA stories over a period of time allows the student to revisit and reread enjoyable accounts of memorable experiences.

### Reading Activity

Give one copy of the LEA story to the student. Direct her to read it silently. Next, ask her to read it aloud. Using the second copy, follow along and identify any sight word miscues with a check mark or circle.

### Postreading Activity

Use the marker to write the sight word miscues on the laminated checkerboard partially filled with additional sight words. Each square on the board should contain a sight word.

Play a game of checkers. Each player attempts to pronounce the word where her checker lands. After playing the game, ask her to read aloud a total of 10 sight words, the majority of which originated from the LEA story.

### Independent Practice

The student will add the 10 sight words to her personal dictionary. She will list the word and write a sentence that contains the word. On returning to class, the personal dictionary will be checked.

### Notes

## Domain and Area of Instruction

Word recognition: Sight vocabulary
Literacy stage: Initial reading

### Intended Learning Outcome

After reading aloud five preselected high-frequency words, the student will write five sentences, each containing one of the words, to the teacher's satisfaction.

## Materials

- High-frequency word flashcards (Gunning, 2000)
- Gelatin powder
- Wax paper
- Blank sentence strips
- Multicolored markers
- Scissors
- Envelopes

## Prereading Activity

Sprinkle powdered gelatin on wax paper. Using high-frequency words written on cards, choose one, pronounce it, and spell it aloud. As the letters are voiced, direct the student to use his finger and write them in the gelatin. When the spelling is complete, repeat the word. Ask the student to pronounce the word. Continue until five words have been written and read.

High-frequency words are 200 words that comprise about 60 percent of the words in continuous text (see Figure 4-2). Because they appear so frequently, they should be thoroughly learned as soon as possible.

## Reading Activity

Pair the student with a partner to play concentration. Place facedown duplicate high-frequency word cards of each of the five previously read words. If the student uncovers two cards that match, he must say the word correctly and use it in a sentence. Then he keeps the two cards. If the cards do not match or if they are mispronounced, he turns the cards facedown and the partner plays. The person holding the most cards wins the game.

On completion of the game, sort the cards so that each student receives five words. Also, give them five blank sentence strips and five different colored markers each. Using a different colored marker for each sentence, direct them to write five sentences, each containing one of the words. Collect the completed sentence strips and, using the scissors, cut the sentence strips word by word. Put all the words written by each student in two envelopes.

## Postreading Activity

Instruct the students to exchange the envelopes and remake the five sentences. After building the sentences, have the original author check them. If the sentence is correct, the assembler will read it aloud. For each correct sentence, one point will be awarded. The student with the most points is the winner.

## Independent Practice

The student will take the envelope containing all the words from his five sentences home. Role-playing the teacher, he will ask a family member or friend to reconstruct the sentences and read them aloud.

| the | had | would | find | same | different | am |
|---|---|---|---|---|---|---|
| of | but | other | use | right | number | us |
| and | what | into | water | look | away | left |
| a | all | has | little | think | again | end |
| to | were | more | long | also | off | along |
| in | when | two | very | around | went | while |
| is | we | her | after | another | tell | sound |
| you | there | like | word | came | men | house |
| that | can | him | called | three | say | might |
| it | an | time | just | word | small | next |
| he | your | see | new | come | every | below |
| for | which | no | where | work | found | saw |
| was | their | could | most | must | still | something |
| on | said | make | almost | part | big | thought |
| are | if | than | get | because | between | both |
| as | will | first | through | does | name | few |
| with | do | been | back | even | should | those |
| his | each | its | much | place | home | school |
| they | about | who | good | old | give | show |
| at | how | now | before | well | air | always |
| be | up | people | go | such | line | looked |
| this | out | my | man | here | mother | large |
| from | then | made | our | take | set | often |
| I | them | over | write | why | world | together |
| have | she | did | sat | things | own | ask |
| not | many | down | me | great | under | turn |
| or | some | way | day | help | last | |
| by | so | only | too | put | read | |
| one | these | may | any | years | never | |

**Figure 4-2.** High-frequency words.

*Source:* From *Creating Literacy Instruction for All Children 3/e* by Thomas G. Gunning. Copyright © 2000, as adapted from *The Educator's Word Frequency Guide* by S. M. Zeno, S. H. Ivens, R. T. Millard, & R. Duvvuri, 1995. Brewster, NY: Touchstone Applied Science Associates. Reprinted by permission of Allyn & Bacon, Boston, MA.

### Suggested Reading

Gunning, T. G. (2000). *Creating literacy instruction for all children* (3rd ed.). Boston: Allyn & Bacon.

### Notes

_____

_____

_____

_____

_____

## Domain and Area of Instruction

Word recognition: Antonyms
Literacy stage: Initial reading

### Intended Learning Outcome

After direct instruction in antonyms, the student will complete in writing a crossword puzzle that focuses on word opposites with 100 percent accuracy.

### Materials

- Worksheet with five sentences, each with an underlined word
- Student-selected poetry
- Crossword puzzle
- Paper and writing instruments

### Prereading Activity

Teach the meaning of **antonym**. Just as synonyms are words that have similar meanings, antonyms are words that express the opposite meanings. Explain that a word may have more than one opposite, and some words do not have an exact opposite.

Assess understanding by instructing the student to orally change the underlined word in a sentence to one that has the opposite meaning, for example, It is a <u>hot</u> morning.

## Reading Activity

Visit the library. Have the student select a poetry book. Ask her to choose a poem that describes something or someone. Let her practice reading it silently and then have her read it aloud. Select words from the poem and ask her to provide an antonym for each.

## Postreading Activity

Direct the student to draw an antonym tree. Given a key word written on the trunk of the tree, have her create leaves by writing words that mean the opposite of the key word. Display the tree when finished.

## Independent Practice

With help from a family member or friend, the student will complete a crossword puzzle that gives attention to antonyms. Upon returning to class, the puzzle will be reviewed.

## Notes

## Domain and Area of Instruction

**W**ord recognition: Sight vocabulary
Literacy stage: Initial reading

### Intended Learning Outcome

Given 10 vocabulary word cards, the student will pronounce them within 10 seconds with 80 percent accuracy.

### Materials

- Vocabulary cards
- Markers
- Shoebox
- Literary selection of teacher's choice

### Prereading Activity

Play the bang game (adapted from Gipe, 1998). First, make word cards with the word of interest on one side and a sentence using the word on the other. For every five cards, make a *bang* card. Place all the cards in a shoebox. Have the students take turns choosing cards, one at a time. If a word card is drawn and the word is pronounced correctly, the student keeps the card. If the word cannot be pronounced or the sentence must be read to pronounce the word, the card is returned to the shoebox. If a bang card is drawn, the player must return *all* word cards to the container. The first player to collect five word cards is the winner. The element of chance enables readers of varying abilities to play together and also provides the necessary repetition of new words.

### Reading Activity

Read aloud the literary selection of your choice. Focus on 10 new words and make word cards. Discuss and display the word cards on the wall or bulletin board.

### Postreading Activity

Continue to play the bang game, adding the new word cards and bang cards to the game bank. When finished, choose 10 word cards and have the student pronounce them.

### Independent Practice

The student will take the shoebox home and play the bang game with a family member or friend.

### Suggested Reading

Gipe, J. P. (1998). *Multiple paths to literacy: Corrective techniques for classroom teachers* (4th ed.). Upper Saddle River, NJ: Prentice-Hall.

### Notes

_____

_____

_____

_____

_____

_____

## Domain and Area of Instruction

**W**ord recognition: Fluency
Literacy stage: Initial reading

### Intended Learning Outcome

The student will narrate a play to the teacher's satisfaction, reading with fluency and expression and setting the stage for the actors to read their respective parts.

### Materials

- Play script
- Tape recorder and blank audiocassette
- Video recording equipment

### Prereading Activity

Choose a play (or story or poem that needs no adaptation to be turned into a script). Assign characters. Give the student the role of narrator. Provide rehearsal time, reinforcing fluency and reading with expression. Suggest using a tape recorder to record the voices, and then self-critique the performance.

### Reading Activity

Direct the students to perform the play. Videotape it.

### Postreading Activity

As a group, view and critique the videotaped performance. Arrange to perform the play for other classes.

### Independent Practice

The student will rehearse at home, reading her part to family members or friends.

### Suggested Reading

Bagert, B. (1992). *Let me be . . . the boss.* Honesdale, PA: Boyds Mills/Wordsong.
Martin, B., Jr., & Archambault, J. (1985). *The ghost-eye tree.* New York: Holt.
Martin, B., Jr., & Archambault, J. (1989). *Chicka chicka boom boom.* New York: Simon & Schuster.

### Notes

_____

_____

_____

_____

_____

## Domain and Area of Instruction

Word recognition: Fluency
Literacy stage: Initial reading

### Intended Learning Outcome

The student will select a story and practice reading it aloud until he is able to read with expression and fluency to the teacher's satisfaction.

## Materials

- Student-selected story or book
- Author's chair

## Prereading Activity

Instruct the student to select a story. Approve the book for content and reading level. There are three reading levels: independent, instructional, and frustration. At the independent level, the reader can read without assistance. At the instructional level, the reader can read if support and instruction are provided. At the frustration level, the reader experiences great difficulty, even with guidance and instruction. For this activity, approve the book at the reader's independent level.

## Reading Activity

Provide time for the student to practice reading the story aloud. Have him read it to several classmates, concentrating on fluency and expression.

## Postreading Activity

Arrange to have the student visit another class. Sitting in the author's chair that is placed in front of the group, he will read aloud his selection. Afterwards, provide time for audience comments and compliments.

## Independent Practice

Prior to the final reading, the student will rehearse his story with family members and friends as the audience.

## Notes

# Domain and Area of Instruction

**W**ord recognition: Punctuation
Literacy stage: Initial reading

## Intended Learning Outcome

While reading aloud, the student will demonstrate knowledge of fluency and end punctuation by using stress and intonation to the teacher's satisfaction.

## Materials

- Baseball
- *Sports Illustrated for Kids*

## Prereading Activity

With a distance of two feet, throw a baseball to the student. Ask the student to toss it back. Repeat. Ask the student to describe the movement of the ball. Repeat the activity at four, six, and eight feet.

Considering the varying distances, ask the student to describe the ball's movements (the short tosses are jerkier than the longer ones). Also alert her to notice what happens when the ball lands in her hand. Draw an analogy to reading a passage aloud. When the ball is in the air, it is like a flowing sentence. When the ball is caught, it is like a period.

## Reading Activity

Using an issue of *Sports Illustrated for Kids*, read aloud a requested selection. Demonstrate and then discuss the stress and intonation patterns represented by the punctuation marks. Identify the punctuation marks and their functions.

Read a sentence aloud and have the student repeat the same sentence. Practice as long as needed. When fluent reading of each sentence is modeled, the student should grasp the relationship between a long throw of a baseball and the smooth flow of speech in a sentence.

## Postreading Activity

Direct the student to read aloud the previously practiced sentences, using stress and intonation appropriately.

### Independent Practice

The student will toss a baseball to a family member at various distances. After playing catch, she will explain how throwing a ball is like reading smoothly. Then she will demonstrate by reading aloud a selection of her choice to the listener.

### Suggested Reading

*Sports illustrated for kids.* Birmingham, AL: Time Magazine.

### Notes

_____

_____

_____

_____

_____

## Domain and Area of Instruction

Word recognition: Word analysis
Literacy stage: Transitional

### Intended Learning Outcome

Using a button to identify the definition of the announced word on the playing board, the student will play vocabulary bingo with 80 percent accuracy.

### Materials

- Vocabulary bingo game (cardboard, markers, rulers, 24 vocabulary words, flashcards, buttons, dictionaries)

### Prereading Activity

Announce that the class will design and play vocabulary bingo. Give each student a large square of cardboard. Providing markers and rulers, instruct them to divide their boards into 25 squares, with the center square representing a free space.

Choose 24 vocabulary words. While you design vocabulary flashcards, direct the class to randomly write the definitions of each term on their boards. Encourage the use of dictionaries.

### Reading Activity

Tell the students that they are to identify the announced word's definition on their game boards by using a button to cover the square. Randomly draw the flashcards and read aloud. To win the game, a student must complete a row—vertically, horizontally, or diagonally.

### Postreading Activity

After new vocabulary terms are introduced, direct the students to design additional definition bingo cards.

### Independent Practice

The student will take the vocabulary bingo game home and play with family members or friends.

### Notes

<br>

<br>

<br>

<br>

<br>

## Domain and Area of Instruction

**W**ord recognition: Vocabulary
Literacy stage: Transitional

### Intended Learning Outcome

The student will select five new terms per chapter from *The Westing Game*, write them in her inspector's notebook, define them, and supply two synonyms for each word with 80 percent accuracy.

## Materials

- Multiple copies of *The Westing Game* (Raskin, 1978)
- *Encyclopedia Brown, Boy Detective* (Sobol, 1979)
- Bulletin board labeled "Wall of Mystery" and "Wall of Evidence" to display terms, clues, and predictions
- Thesauruses
- Index cards
- Writing instruments
- Inspector's notebooks (a teacher- or student-made book that contains blank pages with two sections labeled "Clues" and "Terms")

## Prereading Activity

Read aloud a short chapter from *Encyclopedia Brown, Boy Detective*. Bring into play the clues and predictions necessary to solve the problem in the chapter. Explain that the class will read a mystery and that they will role-play detectives by maintaining an inspector's notebook.

## Reading Activity

Assign students to read silently Chapter 1 in *The Westing Game*. Discuss the chapter.

## Postreading Activity

Using the inspector's notebooks, instruct the detectives to label one section "Terms" and a second section "Clues." Have them record five unknown words from Chapter 1 in the "Terms" section and, using a dictionary, define each. Direct them to record any clues or predictions in the "Clues" section.

Arrange the detectives in threes. Have them share their five new terms, respective definitions, and clues. Direct each student to choose one term from a colleague's notebook, add it to her notebook, and share it with the entire class. Assign her to write the word, its definition, and, using a thesaurus, two synonyms on an index card and post it on the bulletin board labeled "Wall of Mystery."

Request that the trio choose the most important clue, write it on an index card, and post it on the bulletin board labeled "Wall of Evidence."

## Independent Practice

The student will read Chapter 2, choose five new terms, and record and define them in her inspector's notebook. She will also jot down any relevant clues. On returning to class, the detectives will reconvene and further their investigation.

### Suggested Reading

Raskin, E. (1978). *The Westing game.* New York: Dutton.
Sobol, D. J. (1979). *Encyclopedia Brown, boy detective.* New York: Bantam.

### Notes

_____

_____

_____

_____

_____

_____

## Domain and Area of Instruction

**W**ord recognition: Vocabulary
Literacy stage: Transitional

### Intended Learning Outcome

By reading *The Phantom Tollbooth*, the student will increase his vocabulary by choosing two new words per chapter and creating a vocabulary concept web for each to the teacher's satisfaction.

### Materials

- *The Phantom Tollbooth* (Juster, 1989) or book of choice
- Vocabulary notebook
- Writing instruments

### Prereading Activity

Preview the book *The Phantom Tollbooth* with the student. Look at the cover, thumb through the pages, and then brainstorm alternative titles.

## Reading Activity

Assign the student to silently read the book. After he reads each chapter, direct him to choose two new words and record them in his vocabulary notebook.

## Postreading Activity

Review the vocabulary concept web protocol (see Figure 4-3). Select his first word and demonstrate by placing it in the center of a page in the vocabulary notebook. Outlying components are the definition, a synonym, the transcribed sentence from the book that contains the word, and a drawing depicting the meaning of the word. Model by completing the web. Observe as he makes a concept web for the second word. Remind him to repeat this procedure for every chapter read.

## Independent Practice

After reading the book and compiling the vocabulary notebook, the student will choose a minimum of 20 words. Using these, he will create a crossword puzzle that will be shared with the class.

## Suggested Reading

Juster, N. (1989). *The phantom tollbooth*. New York: Alfred A. Knopf.

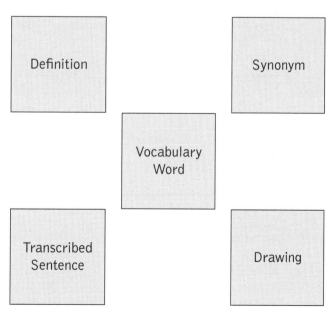

**Figure 4-3.**    Vocabulary concept web protocol.

**Notes**

_____

_____

_____

_____

_____

_____

## Domain and Area of Instruction

**W**ord recognition: Fluency
Literacy stage: Transitional

### Intended Learning Outcome

After listening to a taped reading of Chapters 2 and 3 of _Frindle_, the student
will read them aloud to the teacher's satisfaction.

### Materials

- _Frindle_ (Clements, 1996) or book of choice
- Tape recorder
- Taped reading of Chapters 2 and 3 of _Frindle_
- Materials for chosen project

### Prereading Activity

Introduce the book _Frindle_. Read Chapter 1 aloud to the student. Assign her to
listen to the recording of Chapters 2 and 3 while she reads along silently.

### Reading Activity

Direct the student to read aloud Chapters 2 and 3 with feeling and expression.
Provide comments and encourage discussion.

## Postreading Activity

Have the student choose one of the following projects:

1. Create a collage to describe her favorite character or part of the story.
2. Design a new book jacket.
3. Using movement and pantomime, act out a scene from the story.

Responding to literature through the arts encourages active involvement and individual exploration of text. The reader makes connections and reflects on the reading experience.

## Independent Practice

The student will take both the book and her project home. She will read aloud Chapters 1–3 to a family member or friend.

## Suggested Reading

Clements, A. (1996). *Frindle*. New York: Simon & Schuster.

## Notes

_____

_____

_____

_____

_____

# Domain and Area of Instruction

Word recognition: Context clues
Literacy stage: Transitional

## Intended Learning Outcome

The student will choose and list 10 unknown words from a newspaper article and, using context clues, define them with 80 percent accuracy.

## Materials

- Current newspapers
- Writing instruments
- Paper

## Prereading Activity

Give the student the daily newspaper. Have him survey it for interesting articles. Instruct him to select one article, read it, choose 10 unknown words, and list them on a sheet of paper.

## Reading Activity

Ask the student to read aloud the selected newspaper article. Each time he encounters one of the listed words, let him read to the end of the sentence and then stop. Ask him to define the word. Encourage him to use the surrounding words to figure out its meaning. This is using context clues. Continue until the 10 words have been read and defined.

## Postreading Activity

Direct the student to define each word by using a dictionary. Compare and discuss his definitions with those in the dictionary. Summarize by reinforcing the value of using context clues.

## Independent Practice

For one week the student will read the newspaper and choose five new words. Using both context clues and a dictionary, he will define them.

## Notes

## Domain and Area of Instruction

Word recognition: Fluency
Literacy stage: Transitional

### Intended Learning Outcome

Using the repeated reading strategy, the student will read aloud a passage written at her independent level until 100 percent accuracy in fluency is achieved.

### Materials

- Two copies of a selected passage from *Pioneer Cat* (Hooks, 1998)
- Repeated reading graph
- Colored pencils
- Stopwatch
- Stuffed toy cats, cat stickers, and cat bookmarks

### Prereading Activity

Place on the table toys, stickers, bookmarks, and the book *Pioneer Cat*, all pertaining to cats. Give the student five minutes to explore and interact with the items. Ask, "Do you think the pioneers had cats in the wagons as they traveled westward? Let's find out as we read a passage from *Pioneer Cat*."

### Reading Activity

Describe the repeated reading strategy to the student. Here one reads and rereads aloud a passage until it is read accurately and fluently. First, the reading passage should be at the student's independent level, meaning she can read the selection without assistance. Second, she reads aloud for one minute while the listener times her and charts miscues on the repeated reading graph (see Figure 4-4). Next, the listener discusses the errors and strategies to correct them. The reader silently rereads the passage and then reads aloud for the second time. Again, miscues are charted, but with a different colored pencil. The procedure continues until the reading is fluent.

Apply the repeated reading strategy as the student reads aloud a passage from *Pioneer Cat*.

### Postreading Activity

Make the statement: "Provide evidence that the pioneers took cats in their wagons as they traveled westward." Encourage the student to use the passage to support her answer. Using the chart, discuss improvements in oral reading.

Name _____

### Repeated Reading Graph

| Date | Level | Name of Passage | Number of Words Read in 1 Minute | Number of Miscues |
|------|-------|-----------------|----------------------------------|-------------------|
|      |       |                 |                                  |                   |
|      |       |                 |                                  |                   |
|      |       |                 |                                  |                   |
|      |       |                 |                                  |                   |
|      |       |                 |                                  |                   |
|      |       |                 |                                  |                   |
|      |       |                 |                                  |                   |
|      |       |                 |                                  |                   |
|      |       |                 |                                  |                   |
|      |       |                 |                                  |                   |
|      |       |                 |                                  |                   |
|      |       |                 |                                  |                   |
|      |       |                 |                                  |                   |
|      |       |                 |                                  |                   |
|      |       |                 |                                  |                   |

**Figure 4-4.**    Repeated reading graph.

### Independent Practice

The student will visit the library and choose a book with an animal theme. She will read it aloud to a family member or friend.

### Suggested Reading

Hooks, W. H. (1998). *Pioneer cat.* New York: Random House.

**Notes**

_____

_____

_____

_____

_____

_____

## Domain and Area of Instruction

**W**ord recognition: Context clues
Literacy stage: Transitional

### Intended Learning Outcome

After reading both silently and orally a passage from *The Ghost Cadet*, the student will complete aloud the cloze passage by supplying the missing words with 90 percent accuracy.

### Materials

- *The Ghost Cadet* (Alphin, 1991) or book of choice
- Two copies of the reading passage
- Writing instruments
- Cloze passage based on the reading passage
- Art paper
- Colored pencils

### Prereading Activity

Without showing him the book, read aloud the book title, *The Ghost Cadet*. Ask him to draw a book jacket based on only the title. After he completes the drawing, compare book covers. Discuss similarities and differences.

### Reading Activity

Preselect a passage from *The Ghost Cadet*. Make two copies. Give the student one, and have him read it aloud. On your copy, note any decoding miscues or errors by using check marks.

When he is finished, point out sentences that have miscues. Inquire if they "make sense." Using words surrounding miscues, encourage him to correct them.

### Postreading Activity

Using the previously read passage, prepare a cloze passage. Delete a total of 10 words, choosing from those that were read incorrectly. List the deleted words on a separate sheet of paper. Referring to the list, direct the student to read aloud the cloze passage and supply the missing words.

### Independent Practice

Using a book of his choice, the student will read aloud to a family member or friend for 15 minutes per day.

### Suggested Reading

Alphin, E. M. (1991). *The ghost cadet*. New York: Scholastic.

### Notes

## Domain and Area of Instruction

**W**ord recognition: Listening vocabulary
Literacy stage: Transitional

### Intended Learning Outcome

Given a list of 10 words chosen from a selection about baseball, the student will define them, based on how they were used in the sentence, with 80 percent accuracy.

### Materials

- Book or story with baseball theme
- Vocabulary list
- Paper and writing instruments

### Prereading Activity

Discuss baseball with the student. Draw a baseball diamond. Place the word *baseball* on the pitching mound or center. Record shared details at first base, second base, third base, and in the outfield.

Select a story with a baseball theme to read aloud. Choose 10 words and give the list to the student. Discuss the words briefly.

### Reading Activity

Read aloud the baseball story to the student. Give her the list and request her to listen for the words. When she hears one, direct her to define it, based on how the term was used in the sentence.

### Postreading Activity

Assess the definitions. Discuss the words and their meanings.

### Independent Practice

Using the list of 10 words, the student will write an original story about baseball. On returning to class, she will share it with the teacher.

### Suggested Reading

Christopher, M. (1954). *The lucky baseball bat*. Boston: Little, Brown.
Christopher, M. (1964). *Catcher with a glass arm*. Boston: Little, Brown.
Smith, R. K. (1989). *Bobby Baseball*. New York: Delacorte.

**Notes**

_____

_____

_____

_____

_____

# Domain and Area of Instruction

Word recognition: Context clues
Literacy stage: Basic literacy

### Intended Learning Outcome

Using the social studies textbook, the student will choose 10 unknown words from each assigned chapter and create a word bank to the teacher's satisfaction.

### Materials

- Key ring
- Hole punch
- 3-inch × 5-inch note cards
- Dictionary
- Social studies textbook
- *The Day Fort Sumter Was Fired On: A Photo History of the Civil War* (Haskins, 1995)
- Writing instruments

### Prereading Activity

Read aloud to the class *The Day Fort Sumter Was Fired On: A Photo History of the Civil War* and share the pictures. With the students, survey the Civil War chapter in the social studies textbook. Ask them to examine the headings, subheadings, and pictures. Assign the students to draw a picture and write a paragraph predicting the chapter's contents.

### Reading Activity

Assign the students to read the Civil War chapter silently. While reading, instruct them to select 10 new or unfamiliar words and write each word on a note card.

### Postreading Activity

Arrange the class in fours to share their words. Direct each group to discuss the words, research their definitions, and write them on the back of each note card. The students will punch holes in each note card and add it to their word bank key rings.

### Independent Practice

The student will take his word bank key ring home and review the words with a family member or friend.

### Suggested Reading

Haskins, J. (1995). *The day Fort Sumter was fired on: A photo history of the Civil War*. New York: Scholastic.

### Notes

## Domain and Area of Instruction

**W**ord recognition: Vocabulary
Literacy stage: Basic literacy

### Intended Learning Outcome

The student will expand her meaning vocabulary by 10 new words per book club reading selection. She will write the definition and two synonyms for each word in her literacy journal with 100 percent accuracy.

### Materials

- Book club books
- Dictionary
- Thesaurus
- Literacy journal

### Prereading Activity

If it is financially feasible, introduce the student to a paperback book club. Give her an order form. Encourage her to purchase a selection and expand her personal library.

Publishers of paperback books often manage book clubs for classrooms. The class receives monthly listings of available titles, and students place orders through the teacher. Two resources are Scholastic Book Clubs (555 Broadway, New York, NY 10012–3999) and Troll Book Clubs (100 Corporate Drive, Mahwah, NJ 07430).

### Reading Activity

When the books arrive, distribute them. Direct the student to read for pleasure. Have her list unknown words in a literacy journal.

### Postreading Activity

Using a dictionary and a thesaurus, instruct the student to write a definition and two synonyms for at least 10 of the unknown words listed.

### Independent Practice

The student will use her new words in daily conversations and in writing. Also, she will reinforce vocabulary by playing word games, such as Scrabble.

**Notes**

_____

_____

_____

_____

_____

_____

## Domain and Area of Instruction

**W**ord recognition: Fluency
Literacy stage: Basic literacy

### Intended Learning Outcome

Given a passage from *Where the Red Fern Grows*, the student will prepare a dramatic script, assume the role of the character, and read the script with proper intonation, phrasing, and fluency to the teacher's satisfaction.

### Materials

- *Where the Red Fern Grows* (Rawls, 1961)
- Copies of several transcribed scenes from the book
- Commercial video of the book
- Videocassette player and monitor
- Paper and writing instruments

### Prereading Activity

List the following phrases from *Where the Red Fern Grows* on the board: (1) "as the crow flies," (2) "scattered up along hogback ridge," (3) "in a mile eating trot," and (4) "bushed out like a corn tassel." Have the students draw pictures of the literal translations of these phrases. Share and discuss.

## Reading Activity

Choose several scenes from the book. Based on the number of characters in each scene, arrange the class into groups. Give each group one scene. Direct them to prepare a dramatic script, choose characters, rehearse, and then present their scripts.

## Postreading Activity

View the commercial video of *Where the Red Fern Grows*. Compare the classroom performances to those in the video.

## Independent Practice

The student will make a character web of his character. He will place the character's name in the center of a sheet of paper and then draw lines to the center, spiderweb fashion. On these lines, he will write words that describe the character.

## Suggested Reading

Rawls, W. (1961). *Where the red fern grows*. New York: Doubleday.

## Notes

## Domain and Area of Instruction

**W**ord recognition: Vocabulary
Literacy stage: Basic literacy

### Intended Learning Outcome

Reading a trade book of her choice, the student will list unknown words in her personal dictionary. Using a variety of strategies, she will define the words with 100 percent accuracy.

### Materials

- Copies of selected passages
- Paper and writing instruments
- Personal dictionaries
- Trade books
- Dictionary

### Prereading Activity

Give each student a passage and instruct her to read it silently. Direct her to list any unknown words in her personal dictionary and, without consulting the dictionary, devise definitions. Compare with a partner.

Engage in a discussion about the words' meanings and how they were determined. Context clues, prior knowledge, visual analysis, and structural analysis are possible strategies. Have the student check the accuracy of her definitions by consulting a dictionary.

### Reading Activity

Assign the student to select and read silently a trade book. While reading, she will record unknown words in her personal dictionary.

Trade books are available at bookstores and libraries; they are not textbooks. Those for young adults encompass a wide range of genres, including mystery, adventure, science fiction, romance, supernatural, fantasy, sports, humor, and historical fiction. They often delve into other cultures or explore how others cope with the problems inherent in being a young adult.

### Postreading Activity

Direct the student to define the unknown words in her personal dictionary. Encourage her to use not only the dictionary but also other strategies. Review the personal dictionary periodically.

### Independent Practice

The student will write a book link that introduces her trade book to another person and entices the person to read it. A book link is a brief advertisement that highlights exciting, interesting events in the book. On returning to class, the student will post the book link on the book link bulletin board.

### Notes

_____

_____

_____

_____

_____

## Domain and Area of Instruction

Word recognition: Phonics
Literacy stage: Basic literacy

### Intended Learning Outcome

Given a list of 20 polysyllabic words, the student will pronounce the words and then circle the root words with 80 percent accuracy.

### Materials

- Computer with Internet capabilities and printer
- Internet article about bicycles (or topic of choice)
- Worksheet with polysyllabic words
- Paper, highlighter, and writing instruments

### Prereading Activity

Using the Internet, request the student to search mountain bikes. Encourage him to read information from various links.

### Reading Activity

Instruct him to print an informational article about bicycles. Then, have him highlight words with more than two syllables. From the highlighted words, select those that are good examples of polysyllabic words containing root words. Choosing several, model how to identify the root words by circling them. Discuss.

### Postreading Activity

Select additional polysyllabic words for a total of 20, and list them on a worksheet. Instruct the student to pronounce each word and then circle its root word. Evaluate the answers.

### Independent Practice

The student will choose one of the following activities: create a collage based on the theme of bicycles, read another article or book about bicycles, or draw a bicycle and label its parts.

### Notes

_____

_____

_____

_____

_____

_____

## Domain and Area of Instruction

Word recognition: Structural analysis
Literacy stage: Basic literacy

### Intended Learning Outcome

Given a list of 10 words derived from the Latin words *photo*, *bio*, *graph*, and *auto*, the student will define each word to the teacher's satisfaction.

## Materials

- Board and chalk
- Flashlight
- *English from the Roots Up* (Lundquist, 1989)
- Dictionaries
- Paper and writing instruments
- Handout with English derivatives
- Vocabulary journal

## Prereading Activity

Write the word *photo* on the board and inquire if anyone knows the Latin meaning. List responses. Inform the students that they will watch a short play dramatizing the meaning of the word.

Perform a one-person play, using the word *photo* as an obvious translation to *light*. Arrange for a student to shine a flashlight on you.

Teacher: "Turn off that light. I am photophobic!"
"Pull the blinds; the photo is really bothering me!"
"I wish I had a telephoto lens so I could see the light from far away!"

Again, ask the students to define the word *photo*.

Describe the connection between Greek and Latin words and English. Explain that a key to developing vocabulary is to learn Latin and Greek words. An excellent resource for this activity is *English from the Roots Up*.

## Reading Activity

Write the word *light* on the board. Brainstorm other words that contain the root word *photo*. Elicit the connection between the Latin word and its definition. Direct the students to use their dictionaries to list and define three additional words that contain the root word *photo*.

Repeat this procedure for the Latin words *bio*, *graph*, and *auto*.

## Postreading Activity

Give the students a handout with 10 words derived from the Latin and Greek words that have been studied. Assign the students to underline the root words and then define each term without using the dictionary.

## Independent Practice

The student will consult her dictionary and select five additional words that contain Latin or Greek root words. She will write each word and its definition in her vocabulary journal.

### Suggested Reading

Lundquist, J. K. (1989). *English from the roots up.* Bellevue, WA: Literacy Unlimited.

### Notes

## Domain and Area of Instruction

Word recognition: Vocabulary
Literacy stage: Basic literacy

### Intended Learning Outcome

After reading a descriptive story silently, the student will create a poem containing five vivid words, used in the proper context to the teacher's satisfaction.

### Materials

- Lemon drop candy
- Board and chalk
- Descriptive story (multiple copies)
- Highlighters
- Paper and writing instruments
- Art supplies (construction paper, magazines, markers, glue, tape)
- Thesaurus

### Prereading Activity

Arrange the students into groups. Give each group some lemon drops and encourage them to think about how they look, smell, feel, and taste. Brainstorm words that describe the lemon drops and list them on the board. Reinforce the power of words that describe or modify (adjectives and adverbs).

### Reading Activity

Select a descriptive story and make multiple copies. Distribute to the class. Assign them to read it silently. Afterwards, have them skim the story for vivid language and highlight the words.

### Postreading Activity

Referring to the highlighted words, instruct the students to compose a poem that includes at least five of the descriptive words. Encourage them to use the art supplies to create a visual of the poem.

### Independent Practice

The student will share his poem with a family member or friend. Using a thesaurus, he will list one synonym and one antonym for each of the five descriptive words.

### Notes

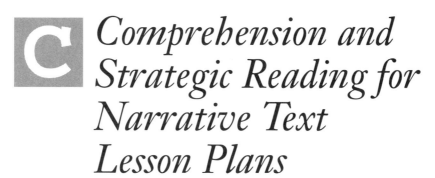

CHAPTER *5*

# Comprehension and Strategic Reading for Narrative Text Lesson Plans

## Domain and Area of Instruction

Comprehension and strategic reading for narrative text: Cause and effect
Literacy stage: Initial reading

### Intended Learning Outcome

Given five cause-and-effect story starters, the student will listen to each cause and then circle the best effect option on a teacher-prepared worksheet with 80 percent accuracy.

### Materials

- Food coloring, glass, and water
- Board and chalk
- Two sets of cause-and-effect worksheets
- Writing instruments
- Puppets

### Prereading Activity

Using the chalkboard, write the words *cause* and *effect*, creating two columns. Under *cause*, write, "mixing yellow and blue food coloring." Ask the students what they think the effect will be when these two colors are mixed. Write the students' responses under the word *effect*. Mix the colors in the glass to demonstrate the results.

### Reading Activity

Read aloud a total of five story starters that deal with cause and effect. Using the worksheet, instruct the student to complete each sentence by circling the appropriate effect; for example, "Jane decided she wanted to go down the hill on her roller skates. She skated so fast . . . she fell and skinned her elbows and knees." Share responses.

### Postreading Activity

Invite the students to use puppets to dramatize the events described on the cause-and-effect worksheet.

### Independent Practice

Given a second worksheet with five cause-and-effect scenarios, the student will circle the effect option that best completes the story starter. On returning to school, the responses will be discussed.

### Notes

_____

_____

_____

_____

_____

_____

## Domain and Area of Instruction

Comprehension and strategic reading for narrative text: Listening
Literacy stage: Initial reading

### Intended Learning Outcome

After listening to a description of a dinosaur, the student will write five sentences describing the dinosaur with 80 percent accuracy.

### Materials

- Dinosaur literature
- Paper and writing instruments

### Prereading Activity

Provide a variety of books dealing with dinosaurs, and ask the student to choose one. Read the book to him.

### Reading Activity

Read aloud a description of a dinosaur. Possible selections are *The Trouble with Tyrannosaurus Rex* (Cauley, 1988) and *Dinosaur Encore* (Mullins, 1993).

### Postreading Activity

Direct the student to write five sentences describing the dinosaur. Share and discuss.

### Independent Practice

The student will draw a picture of the dinosaur of his choice. On returning to class, the drawing will be posted on a bulletin board.

### Suggested Reading

Cauley, L. B. (1988). *The trouble with Tyrannosaurus Rex*. San Diego: Harcourt Brace.
Mullins, P. (1993). *Dinosaur encore*. New York: HarperCollins/Putnam.

**Notes**

_____

_____

_____

_____

_____

## Domain and Area of Instruction

Comprehension and strategic reading for narrative text:
    Comprehension monitoring
Literacy stage: Initial reading

### Intended Learning Outcome

Given two stories and a Venn diagram, with teacher assistance, the student will pinpoint the common and unique story elements by writing them in the correct section of the Venn diagram to the teacher's satisfaction.

### Materials

- Teacher-made interest survey related to stuffed animals
- Story charts
- Writing instruments
- Board and chalk
- *The Velveteen Rabbit* (Williams, 1922)
- *The Adventures of Pinocchio* (Collodi, 1988)

### Prereading Activity

Have the students complete a five-question interest survey related to the theme of stuffed animals. Arrange the class into groups and direct them to share their responses.

Introduce and distribute the story chart. Discuss its four sections: characters, setting, vocabulary, and questions (see Figure 5-1). Inform the students that they will be listening to two stories and completing a story chart for each.

Name _____ Title _____

## Story Chart

| Characters | Setting | Vocabulary | Questions |
|---|---|---|---|
|  |  |  |  |

**Figure 5-1.**   Story chart protocol.

### Reading Activity

Read aloud *The Velveteen Rabbit*, encouraging volunteers to assist in the reading. Periodically, ask relevant questions and promote student questioning. When applicable, stop and direct the students to write information in the relevant column of the story chart.

After reading the story, review the story chart, answering questions and defining vocabulary.

Read aloud *The Adventures of Pinocchio*. Using a second story chart, follow the same procedure.

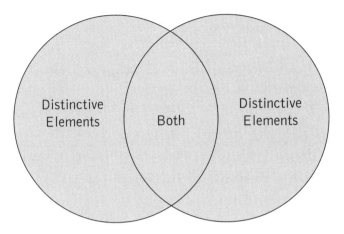

**Figure 5-2.**   Venn diagram protocol.

## Postreading Activity

Draw a Venn diagram on the board (see Figure 5-2). Explain the various sections. If an element is common to both stories, place it in the overlapping section of the circles. If an element applies to one story only, place it in the circle for that story.

Using data from the two story charts, compare *The Velveteen Rabbit* and *The Adventures of Pinocchio* by filling in the appropriate sections of the Venn diagram. After demonstrating, encourage student participation.

## Independent Practice

The student will choose to either draw a picture of her favorite stuffed animal or write an original story or poem that relates to animals.

## Suggested Reading

Collodi, C. (Translator E. Harden). (1988). *The adventures of Pinocchio.* New York: Knopf.
Williams, M. (1922). *The velveteen rabbit.* New York: Doubleday.

## Notes

_____

_____

_____

_____

## Domain and Area of Instruction

Comprehension and strategic reading for narrative text:
    Recreational reading
Literacy stage: Initial reading

### Intended Learning Outcome

Using a Books I Would Like to Read journal, the student will select and list a variety of books to the teacher's satisfaction.

### Materials

- Books I Would Like to Read journal
- Writing instruments

### Prereading Activity

Explain that choosing books to read is an important skill to learn. Demonstrate how to preview a book by looking at the cover, reading the author's name, and flipping through the pages.

Next, demonstrate the thumb test to determine if the book is too easy or difficult to read. Choose a page and read it aloud. Explain that every time the reader meets an unknown word, he extends one finger. If the reader puts up his thumb or counts five words, the book is too difficult. If no fingers are raised, the book may be too easy to read.

Provide time for the student to visit the school library and select a book. Have him record the book's title in his Books I Would Like to Read journal.

### Reading Activity

During silent reading time, direct the student to read his book. Arrange a conference when he will read aloud for three minutes. Monitor his reading and book selection.

### Postreading Activity

When he is finished, direct him to place a check mark after the book title in the journal, return the book, and choose another. Likewise, he will add the new title to his journal and read the book.

### Independent Practice

The student will continue to select books and add the titles to his Books I Would Like to Read journal. When he has read the book, he will place a check mark after the title.

### Notes

_____

_____

_____

_____

_____

_____

## Domain and Area of Instruction

Comprehension and strategic reading for narrative text:
  Listening comprehension
Literacy stage: Initial reading

### Intended Learning Outcome

After listening to a predictable story such as *Stone Soup* (McGovern, 1971), the student will orally answer questions about the story with 80 percent accuracy.

### Materials

- Predictable story (one with anticipated or repeated words)
- Paper and writing instruments

## Prereading Activity

Choose a predictable story. Share the title and book cover with the students. Give them time to guess what the book is about with a buddy. Share responses.

## Reading Activity

Read the story aloud to the students. Use an enthusiastic voice to emphasize the predictable parts. Pause occasionally and ask the students to paraphrase the story line.

## Postreading Activity

After reading, ask the students, "What made the story predictable?" Ask additional questions, and if 80 percent comprehension is not evident, reread the story. Then instruct the students to act out the predictable parts of the story.

Introduce the students to additional predictable books: *Annie and the Wild Animals* (Brett, 1985); *The Lock, the Mouse, and the Little Red Hen* (Cauley, 1982); *The House That Jack Built* (Guilfoile, 1962); *The Jacket I Wear in the Snow* (Neitzel, 1989); *Busy Monday Morning* (Nomaska, 1985); *Roll Over!* (Peek, 1981); *The Z Was Zapped* (Van Allsburg, 1987); and *Alexander and the Terrible, Horrible, No Good, Very Bad Day* (Viorst, 1976). Allow time for surveying.

## Independent Practice

The student will select a predictable book, practice reading it aloud, and then read it to family members or friends.

## Suggested Reading

Brett, J. (1985). *Annie and the wild animals.* Boston: Houghton Mifflin.
Cauley, L. B. (1982). *The lock, the mouse, and the little red hen.* New York: Putnam.
Guilfoile, E. (1962). *The house that Jack built.* New York: Holt, Rinehart, & Winston.
McGovern, A. (1971). *Stone soup.* New York: Scholastic.
Neitzel, S. (1989). *The jacket I wear in the snow.* New York: Greenwillow.
Nomaska, J. (1985). *Busy Monday morning.* New York: Greenwillow.
Peek, M. (1981). *Roll over!* Boston: Houghton Mifflin.
Van Allsburg, C. (1987). *The z was zapped.* Boston: Houghton Mifflin.
Viorst, J. (1976). *Alexander and the terrible, horrible, no good, very bad day.* New York: Atheneum.

**Notes**

_____

_____

_____

_____

_____

## Domain and Area of Instruction

Comprehension and strategic reading for narrative text: Details
Literacy stage: Initial reading

### Intended Learning Outcome

Using a worksheet that contains five spokes of a wheel that extend from the story title, the student will write story details on the spokes with 80 percent accuracy.

### Materials

- Selection of children's literature
- Board and chalk
- Worksheet
- Paper and writing instruments

### Prereading Activity

Read aloud a short story. Direct the student to listen for details. After the reading, draw a wheel with spokes on the board. Write the title of the story in the center of the wheel. Have the student state details and write one detail per spoke.

### Reading Activity

Assign the student to read silently a story at his independent level. Remind him to read for details.

## Postreading Activity

Give the student a worksheet containing a wheel with five spokes. Supply the title of the story in the center of the wheel. Tell the student to fill in the five spokes with five details from the story. Discuss.

## Independent Practice

The student will design his own wheel, choosing the number of spokes. He will read a story of his choice, fill in details on the spokes, and then retell the story to a family member or friend.

## Notes

_____

_____

_____

_____

_____

# Domain and Area of Instruction

Comprehension and strategic reading for narrative text: Sequencing
Literacy stage: Initial reading

## Intended Learning Outcome

Given 10 events from a story read aloud by the teacher, the student will sequence the events by numbering them from 1 to 10 with 100 percent accuracy.

## Materials

- Children's literature
- Worksheet
- Paper and writing instruments

### Prereading Activity

Read aloud a short story to the student. Ask her to state important events from the story and write them on a sheet of paper. Draw a short line in front of each event. Ask the student which event happened first, and have her place a 1 on the line in front of the event. Continue numbering until all the events are in order.

### Reading Activity

Give the student a book written at her independent level, the level at which she requires no assistance with reading. Have her read it silently. Remind her to pay special attention to the order in which events occur in the story.

### Postreading Activity

Give the student a list of 10 randomly ordered events from the story. Allowing her to use the book, instruct her to sequence the events by numbering them from 1 to 10. Evaluate the worksheet and discuss.

### Independent Practice

The student will choose a book to read. After reading it, she will make a worksheet that randomly lists five events from the story. Next, she will devise the answer key. On returning to school, the students will exchange books and their worksheets. After reading the story and completing its worksheet, the reader will consult the student with the key. Together they will score the worksheet.

### Notes

_____

_____

_____

_____

_____

_____

## Domain and Area of Instruction

Comprehension and strategic reading for narrative text: Sequencing
Literacy stage: Initial reading

### Intended Learning Outcome

Given 10 sentences from a story read aloud or silently by the student, he will paste the sentences on the construction paper in the order in which they occurred in the story with 100 percent accuracy.

### Materials

- Comic strips
- Scissors
- Construction paper
- Short story or book
- Story sentences based on sequenced events from the short story or book
- Glue
- Writing instruments

### Prereading Activity

Show the student several comic strips. Read them together; then cut one of the strips into its individual frames. Model how to reconstruct the comic strip and glue it on the construction paper. Working together, cut, arrange, and paste a second comic strip. Finally, ask the student to perform the activity independently.

### Reading Activity

Assign the student to read a short story or book at a level requiring no assistance. Remind him to focus on the order of the events in the story.

### Postreading Activity

Write 10 sentences from the story, one per strip of paper. Have the student arrange them in order and glue them to the construction paper. Read and discuss.

### Independent Practice

At home, the student will observe an event that involves sequencing, such as his parent preparing dinner. He will write simple sentences listing the order of the events. On returning to class, he will read and dramatize the event.

**Notes**

_____

_____

_____

_____

_____

_____

## Domain and Area of Instruction

Comprehension and strategic reading for narrative text:
Main ideas and supporting details
Literacy stage: Transitional

### Intended Learning Outcome

Given 10 short paragraphs, each containing a sentence that does not pertain to the main idea, the student will cross out the inappropriate sentence with 90 percent accuracy.

### Materials

- Worksheet
- Short story
- Paper and writing instruments

### Prereading Activity

Read a story to the student. After reading the story, review each paragraph and ask, What is the main idea of the paragraph? What ideas support the main idea? Where is the main idea frequently found? What are key words that introduce details? Reinforce the concept of main idea and supporting details by drawing a tree whose trunk represents the main idea and whose branches represent details.

### Reading Activity

Assign the student to silently read a short story. For designated paragraphs, have her draw a tree, labeling the main ideas on the trunks and the supporting details on the branches. Review and discuss.

### Postreading Activity

Give the student 10 short paragraphs, each containing one sentence that does not relate to the main idea. Instruct her to cross out the 10 inappropriate sentences. Evaluate and discuss.

### Independent Practice

The student will write a creative short story. She will draw a main idea tree trunk and supporting detail branches for each of five paragraphs.

### Notes

_____

_____

_____

_____

_____

_____

## Domain and Area of Instruction

**C**omprehension and strategic reading for narrative text: Vocabulary
Literacy stage: Transitional

### Intended Learning Outcome

The student will construct a survival guide based on the novel *Hatchet*. The guide will include instructions for using a compass, first aid information, and important telephone numbers.

## Materials

- *Hatchet* (Paulsen, 1987)
- Butcher paper
- Markers
- Small notebooks
- Writing instruments

## Prereading Activity

Tell the students to examine the cover of the book. Ask how old they think the boy on the cover is. After reading the question at the lower right hand corner, ask, "What can you guess about the airplane?" Inquire why the boy might use the hatchet. Ask what kind of animal is illustrated. Ask what they think a silver circle showing three figures means. Given the following clues about the cover, assign the students to write a paragraph predicting what they think will happen in the story.

## Reading Activity

Assign the students to read the first chapter. Divide the class into groups of three students each. Ask the students to think about times when they have been afraid and times when they have been brave. Give them a large piece of butcher paper and instruct them to divide it into six columns. Label the first column "Chapter," the second column "Not Afraid," the third "Learning to Be Brave," the fourth "Trying to Be Brave," the fifth "Afraid," and the sixth column "Terrified." After reading each chapter, instruct the groups to complete the columns. Arrange a panel discussion to share their observations.

## Postreading Activity

Providing small notebooks, ask the groups to design a survival booklet. The booklet must include instructions for using a compass, first aid information, and important phone numbers.

## Independent Practice

The student will read one of his favorite chapters to a family member. He will formulate and ask relevant questions based on making predictions, survival skills, or the listener's feelings and emotions.

## Suggested Reading

Paulsen, G. (1987). *Hatchet.* New York: Bradbury.

**Notes**

_____

_____

_____

_____

_____

# Domain and Area of Instruction

Comprehension and strategic reading for narrative text: Inference
Literacy stage: Transitional

### Intended Learning Outcome

Given a worksheet containing 10 multiple-choice, text-implicit questions, the student will circle the best option with 90 percent accuracy.

### Materials

- *Alexander and the Terrible, Horrible, No Good, Very Bad Day* (Viorst, 1976)
- Student journals
- Worksheet with 10 multiple-choice inference questions
- Paper and writing instruments

### Prereading Activity

Discuss the two levels of comprehension. Level 1 is text-explicit comprehension; the reader acquires the facts of a passage directly from the text as stated by the author. Level 2 is text-implicit comprehension; the reader must think about her answers because the author does not explicitly state them and the answers vary, depending on each respondent's experiential background.

Read phrases aloud and ask text-implicit questions; for example, "Tommy is outside raking the leaves in his yard. What season is it? What words in the phrase make you think that?" Continue until the students demonstrate success.

## Reading Activity

Assign the students to silently read *Alexander and the Terrible, Horrible, No Good, Very Bad Day*. When they are finished, have them write responses to the following two questions in their student journals:

1. What was Alexander's attitude at the beginning of the day?
2. What in the story makes you think that?

## Postreading Activity

Give the students the multiple-choice worksheet and instruct them to answer the 10 text-implicit questions by circling the best option. When they are finished, form groups of no more than four students and have them compare their answers. Encourage discussion and explanations for their choices.

## Independent Practice

The student will conduct an interview with a family member or friend. She will record facts about the person's occupation but not reveal the name of the occupation. Next, she will choose four facts that describe the job and write them on a piece of paper or fact sheet.

On returning to class, the fact sheets will be displayed on a bulletin board. Host a contest in which the students identify the various occupations.

## Suggested Reading

Viorst, J. (1976). *Alexander and the terrible, horrible, no good, very bad day.* New York: Atheneum.

## Notes

## Domain and Area of Instruction

Comprehension and strategic reading for narrative text: Time order
Literacy stage: Transitional

### Intended Learning Outcome

Given five random events from a chapter in *Charlotte's Web*, the student will create a time line and order the events with 100 percent accuracy.

### Materials

- *Charlotte's Web* (White, 1952)
- Board and chalk
- Construction paper, scissors, markers, staplers

### Prereading Activity

Take a field trip to a local farm. Ask the farmer to describe his chores and responsibilities, in order, from morning until night. Engage the students in some of the chores.

### Reading Activity

Read aloud Chapter 1 in *Charlotte's Web*. Brainstorm five random events from Chapter 1. List them on the board and then arrange them in order. Compare events in the story with the field trip.

### Postreading Activity

Using the bulletin board, create a time line. Write each event on a strip of construction paper and staple it in the correct order.

After reading each chapter, repeat the activity. As the story progresses, assign various groups to construct the time lines.

### Independent Practice

Over a weekend, the student will compile a time line based on 10 of his daily activities. They will be listed in chronological or time order. On returning to school, the events will be discussed.

### Suggested Reading

White, E. B. (1952). *Charlotte's web*. New York: Harper & Row.

**Notes**

_____

_____

_____

_____

_____

# Domain and Area of Instruction

Comprehension and strategic reading for narrative text: Listening
Literacy stage: Transitional

### Intended Learning Outcome

After listening to 10 sentences containing 10 to 12 words each, the student will
repeat the sentences with 80 percent accuracy.

### Materials

- Tape recorder and recorded message on audiocassette
- Blocks
- Ten sentences with 10–12 words each

### Prereading Activity

Have the student listen to a recorded message. After listening once, ask her to
retell the message. Together, listen to the message a second time. Discuss
points remembered and those omitted. Further discuss the challenges of listening for details.

### Reading Activity

Sit back-to-back with the student. Give her a set of blocks of different shapes
and colors. Provide directions regarding arranging the blocks. She will listen
and arrange the blocks accordingly. Check the arrangement. Continue the
activity, extending the complexity of directions. Switch roles.

### Postreading Activity

Using prepared sentences of 10–12 words each, read one aloud. Direct her to repeat the sentence. Continue until 10 sentences have been read and repeated.

### Independent Practice

The student will play "telephone" with a group of friends or family members. Starting with short, three-word sentences, she will whisper the message into the next person's ear. This person will relate what was heard to the next person and so on. The last person to listen to the message will say it aloud to discover if repetition changed the wording. Continue with increasingly longer sentences. The student will note the longest sentence that was repeated without error.

### Notes

---

## Domain and Area of Instruction

Comprehension and strategic reading for narrative text: Prediction
Literacy stage: Transitional

### Intended Learning Outcome

Based on the title of the book, the student will predict and write five details he anticipates in the story to the teacher's satisfaction.

### Materials

- Short story
- Board and chalk

- Book of choice
- Paper and writing instruments
- Current newspaper

## Prereading Activity

Introduce a short story by reading the title. By title alone, brainstorm anticipated details and write them on the board. Read the story aloud to the student. Then place a check by the details that occurred.

## Reading Activity

Write the title of the book to be read on the board. Have the student write five anticipated details on a sheet of paper. Assign the student to read the book silently.

## Postreading Activity

When he is finished, have the student reread his anticipated details and place a check by those that occurred. Direct him to support each checked detail by adding the page number where it took place. Discuss responses and justifications.

## Independent Practice

With assistance from family members, the student will anticipate details based on various newspaper headlines. After they mutually read the article, they will validate the details.

## Notes

## Domain and Area of Instruction

Comprehension and strategic reading for narrative text:
Recreational reading
Literacy stage: Transitional

### Intended Learning Outcome

Based on interests, the teacher and student will each select a trade book and read it over a two-week period.

### Materials

- Interest survey
- Books
- Reading log
- Writing instruments

### Prereading Activity

Design an interest survey. Sample questions are:

1. What is your favorite subject?
2. If it were a rainy day, what would you do?
3. What is your favorite animal?
4. If you could be any living thing, what would it be?
5. What is your favorite hobby?
6. If I gave you $100, what would you purchase?

With the student, complete the surveys; compare responses. Then visit the library and each choose a book to read for pleasure.

### Reading Activity

Over a two-week period, read the selected books. Periodically discuss elements of the stories, including characters, plot, favorite parts, and setting.

### Postreading Activity

Host a shareback. Here, readers form a consensus or draw conclusions about the incidents and characters in their books. Also, introduce the reading log (see Figure 5-3), on which students list books read and review them by using the rating key. Complete accordingly.

Name _____

| Book Title | Rating |
|---|---|
|  |  |
|  |  |
|  |  |
|  |  |
|  |  |
|  |  |
|  |  |
|  |  |
|  |  |
|  |  |
|  |  |
|  |  |
|  |  |
|  |  |
|  |  |
|  |  |
|  |  |

*Rating Key*

A = easy to read        1 = very enjoyable
B = average to read     2 = fairly interesting
C = difficult to read   3 = did not like

**Figure 5-3.**   Reading log.

### Independent Practice

The student will maintain the reading log, listing titles and ratings of books read for recreation.

### Notes

_____

_____

_____

_____

_____

_____

## Domain and Area of Instruction

Comprehension and strategic reading for narrative text:
      Recreational reading
Literacy stage: Transitional

### Intended Learning Outcome

The student will select a trade book to read for recreation. He will promote the book to his classmates to the teacher's satisfaction.

### Materials

- Trade books
- Reader response journal
- Writing instruments

### Prereading Activity

Based on the student's interest, visit the library or provide a selection of trade books. Together, survey the books, discuss them briefly, and ask the student to choose one. Compliment his choice.

### Reading Activity

Assign the student to read the book independently. Periodically engage in a student–teacher discussion. Share thoughts, personal experiences, and impressions related to the story line.

### Postreading Activity

Direct the student to present a commercial that "sells" the trade book to his classmates. This will include highlights from the story and reasons for reading it.

### Independent Practice

The student will read independently for at least 30 minutes per day. Afterwards, he will write a response to what was read in his reader response journal. Periodically, he will share the responses with his classmates.

### Notes

_____

_____

_____

_____

_____

## Domain and Area of Instruction

Comprehension and strategic reading for narrative text: Details
Literacy stage: Basic literacy

### Intended Learning Outcome

Given four paragraphs in which one detail in each paragraph does not relate, the student will circle the main idea, underline one supporting detail, and cross out the irrelevant detail in at least three of the four paragraphs.

## Materials

- Trade books
- Transcription of four paragraphs, each with an added irrelevant detail
- Writing instruments

## Prereading Activity

Transcribe a paragraph from a trade book. The paragraph should contain a clear main idea and supporting details. Add one unrelated detail. For example:

> On the desk near the window there's a Castle yearbook. The year my father graduated. *Knights and Dayze.* I haven't looked at it yet. My father's picture is inside, of course, with the pictures of all his classmates, but I don't want to look at his picture. **My favorite drink is Pepsi.** Not yet. I haven't seen him since the bridge because I don't want him seeing me. I'm afraid to even look at his picture because his eyes will be looking into mine. And I know I couldn't face those eyes even in a prep school yearbook. (Cormier, 1979, p. 11)

Demonstrate how to circle the main idea, underline at least one supporting detail, and cross out the one unrelated detail.

## Reading Activity

Transcribe four paragraphs from a variety of trade books. Direct the student to read them silently.

## Postreading Activity

Assign the student to circle the main idea, underline at least one supporting detail, and cross out the one unrelated detail in each paragraph. Evaluate together.

## Independent Practice

The student will listen to a commercial, either on television or on the radio, and take notes. She will later report the main idea and at least one detail about the ad.

## Suggested Reading

Cormier, R. (1979). *After the first death*. New York: Pantheon.

**Notes**

_____

_____

_____

_____

_____

_____

## Domain and Area of Instruction

Comprehension and strategic reading for narrative text: Sequence
Literacy stage: Basic literacy

### Intended Learning Outcome

After reading a chapter from *Castle in the Attic*, the student will answer questions about sequence relationships to the teacher's satisfaction.

### Materials

- Overhead projector and screen
- K-W-L chart transparency and handouts (adapted from Ogle, 1986)
- Overhead projector pens
- *Castle in the Attic* (Winthrop, 1985)
- Writing instruments

### Prereading Activity

Begin the lesson by asking the students what they know and what they want to know about castles. Using an overhead projector pen, record their responses on the K-W-L chart transparency (see Figure 5-4).

Introduce *Castle in the Attic*. Inform them that they will be answering questions about sequence relationships, or time relationships between two or more events.

**Reading Activity**

Divide the class into groups. Within each group, have them read aloud Chapter 1, with each student contributing to the reading. Rove the classroom to monitor progress.

Name _____

## K-W-L Chart

What I know:

What I want to know:

What I learned:

**Figure 5-4.**    K-W-L chart.

*Source:* Adapted from D. M. Ogle (1986). A teaching model that develops active reading of expository text. *The Reading Teacher, 39,* 564–570. Copyright © 1986 by the International Reading Association. Used by permission of the International Reading Association.

### Postreading Activity

Ask questions to initiate a discussion about sequence relationships. Include these:

1. When did _____ take place?
2. What happened before _____?
3. Did _____ happen before or after _____?

### Independent Practice

Given a K-W-L chart handout, the student will write responses in the "What I learned" section. In class, these will be reviewed.

### Suggested Reading

Winthrop, E. (1985). *Castle in the attic.* New York: Putnam.

### Notes

_____

_____

_____

_____

_____

_____

## Domain and Area of Instruction

**C**omprehension and strategic reading for narrative text: Vocabulary
Literacy stage: Basic literacy

### Intended Learning Outcome

After reading four chapters in the book *Magic Tree House #6: Afternoon on the Amazon*, the student will complete a worksheet assessing content-specific vocabulary with 90 percent accuracy.

## Materials

- Anticipation guides
- *Magic Tree House #6: Afternoon on the Amazon* (Osborne, 1995)
- *Terror in the Tropics: The Army Ants* (Lisker, 1977)
- *An Adventure in the Amazon* (Cousteau Society, 1991)
- Globe
- Writing instruments
- Dictionary
- Teacher-prepared vocabulary worksheet

## Prereading Activity

Introduce the topic of rain forests by distributing an anticipation guide to each student. An anticipation guide consists of three to five statements that challenge prereading beliefs. The student responds positively or negatively to each statement and writes her justification for each, so she will have a reference point for discussion. Complete and discuss.

Together, skim *An Adventure in the Amazon* to glean ideas about the tribal people, animals, and vegetation that exist in the Amazon area. Use the globe to locate the Amazon. Browse through *Terror in the Tropics: The Army Ants* to provide background knowledge regarding army ants.

Introduce *Magic Tree House #6: Afternoon on the Amazon* by looking at the front cover and reading the information on the back cover. Ask the students to speculate about the contents of the book. Thumb through the book and read the prologue together.

## Reading Activity

Assign the students to read silently the first four chapters of the book. Instruct them to write down unknown words they encounter and their respective page numbers.

## Postreading Activity

Have the students retell what they read in the first four chapters. For each unknown word recorded, instruct the student to use the dictionary and define it. Also direct her to locate the word in context and reread the sentence for meaning. Finally, assess new vocabulary learned by making a vocabulary worksheet and assigning the student to complete it. Evaluate accordingly.

### Independent Practice

The student will complete reading *Magic Tree House #6: Afternoon on the Amazon*. She will review her anticipation guide responses and note any changes in thinking.

### Suggested Reading

Cousteau Society. (1991). *An adventure in the Amazon*. New York: Simon & Schuster.

Lisker, T. (1977). *Terror in the tropics: The army ants*. New York: Contemporary Perspectives.

Osborne, M. (1995). *Magic tree house #6: Afternoon on the Amazon*. New York: Scholastic.

### Notes

_____

_____

_____

_____

_____

_____

## Domain and Area of Instruction

Comprehension and strategic reading for narrative text: Story elements
Literacy stage: Basic literacy

### Intended Learning Outcome

After reading *Holes*, the student will create a story map that includes the setting, major characters, and plot development in sequence to the teacher's satisfaction.

### Materials

- *Holes* (Sachar, 1998) or book of choice
- Paper and writing instruments

### Prereading Activity

Analyze the book's front and back covers and read the preface. Predict story elements: setting, plot, theme, characters, and conflict.

### Reading Activity

Assign the student to read the book silently. After reading each chapter, have him retell the story.

### Postreading Activity

After he completes the book, direct him to make a story map on a sheet of paper. This will consist of descriptions of the setting and major characters and a summary of the plot development in sequence. Collect and review.

### Independent Practice

The student will draw pictures or sketches of the setting or major characters. When he returns to class, they will be posted on a bulletin board.

### Suggested Reading

Sachar, L. (1998). *Holes*. New York: Farrar, Straus & Giroux.

### Notes

# Domain and Area of Instruction

**C**omprehension and strategic reading for narrative text: Vocabulary
Literacy stage: Basic literacy

## Intended Learning Outcome

Working in pairs and writing in their reader response journals, the students
will use a class-generated list of 20 vocabulary words to create five word categories that are based on the similarities, differences, meanings, and other dis-
tinguishing characteristics of the words.

## Materials

- Board and chalk
- *The Legend of Scarface: A Blackfeet Indian Tale* (San Souci, 1978) or book
  of choice
- Dictionaries
- Reader response journals
- Paper and writing instruments
- Teacher-selected word list

## Prereading Activity

Begin by defining *category* as a subgrouping of items with similar characteristics, qualities, meanings, or functions. Define *sorting* as a process of organizing
items by assigning them to different category groupings.

Lead the class in a sorting activity. Using items found in students' desks,
ask each student to choose one item. Collect the items and place them on a
table so the students can survey them and consider possible categories. Write
on the board "Items Found in Students' Desks" as the broad heading. Next,
ask each student to write one category based on the words on a piece of paper.
Call on students to share their categories and indicate which items are
included in the category. Point out that the categories are not discrete; some
items fit into a number of categories.

## Reading Activity

Request students to read with a partner the book *The Legend of Scarface* and to
generate a list of 10 unknown words encountered in the text. With partner
reading, two students read a selection together. The reading is performed
orally, silently, or both ways.

After reading, have the pairs write their word lists on the board. Compose
a master list of 20 vocabulary words based on the frequency of words cited.

Using a dictionary, assign them to define specified words on the master list in terms of parts of speech, number of syllables, meanings, and morphology. Share the findings.

## Postreading Activity

Using the master list, direct each pair to sort the words into five categories. Explain and discuss. Emphasize that words have special characteristics, just as objects do, and these characteristics assist in the meanings and functions of the words we read.

## Independent Practice

Using a list of 10 teacher-selected words, the student will sort them into three categories. She will use a dictionary to clarify meanings and other defining traits.

## Suggested Reading

San Souci, R. D. (1978). *The legend of Scarface: A Blackfeet Indian tale*. Garden City, NY: Doubleday.

## Notes

# Domain and Area of Instruction

Comprehension and strategic reading for narrative text: Inference
Literacy stage: Basic literacy

### Intended Learning Outcome

After listening to the teacher read pages 18 and 19 from *Reggie Jackson*, the student will label 10 teacher-generated questions as either an inference question or a detail question by writing either *I* or *D* next to each one with 90 percent accuracy.

### Materials

- *Reggie Jackson* (Vass, 1979) or book of choice
- Handouts of pages 18–19 of book
- Handouts with 10 comprehension questions
- Writing instruments

### Prereading Activity

Inform the students of a secret for answering comprehension test questions that is easy and improves performance. Ask if they want to learn it. The secret is recognizing the kind of question being asked.

Define the two types of questions: detail (uses words directly from the text) and inference (uses information from the text as well as the reader's prior knowledge). Practice categorizing questions with examples written on the board.

### Reading Activity

Read aloud pages 18 and 19 from *Reggie Jackson*. Instruct the students to listen carefully because they will label questions as detail or inference afterwards.

### Postreading Activity

Distribute a handout of 10 comprehension questions based on the passage. Instruct the students to label each question as either *I* for inference or *D* for detail. Next, give them the hard copy of the passage. Have them underline each sentence that supports a detailed question and circle the words that are common to both the question and the answer. Based on their findings, encourage corrections. On completion, discuss their responses and compare detail and inference types of questions.

### Independent Practice

Based on an assigned reading, the student will write a total of five inference and detail questions and make a separate answer key. On returning to class, he will give the questions to a classmate who will identify them as *D* or *I*. Using the key, they will assess the answers.

### Suggested Reading

Vass, G. (1979). *Reggie Jackson*. Chicago: Children's Press.

### Notes

_____

_____

_____

_____

_____

_____

## Domain and Area of Instruction

Comprehension and strategic reading for narrative text: Details
Literacy stage: Basic literacy

### Intended Learning Outcome

Using details from *The Korean Cinderella* and *The Egyptian Cinderella*, the student will analyze 10 student-generated phrases and write them in the appropriate sections of a Venn diagram with 80 percent accuracy.

### Materials

- Books with Cinderella theme
- Books and pictures about Korea and Egypt
- *The Korean Cinderella* (Climo, 1993)
- *The Egyptian Cinderella* (Climo, 1989)
- World map or globe
- Butcher paper

- Markers
- Writing instruments
- Handouts of Venn diagram
- Handouts of student-generated phrases

## Prereading Activity

Display books with Cinderella themes and nonfiction books about Korea and Egypt on a table in the classroom. Exhibit pictures depicting the culture, landscape, and people of Korea and Egypt. Find the two countries on the world map or globe. Allocate time for the students to share books and comments.

Discuss the typical Disney version of Cinderella. Tell the students they will be listening to two different books about Cinderella, and encourage them to pay attention to the details.

## Reading Activity

Read aloud *The Korean Cinderella*. Ask questions that compare the story with the Disney version. Record responses relating to the book on the left side of a piece of butcher paper folded in half. Label this side *The Korean Cinderella*.

Label the right side of the butcher paper *The Egyptian Cinderella*. During the oral reading of this book, ask questions that compare the two books. Record responses where applicable on the butcher paper. Using a marker, draw a Venn diagram on another sheet of butcher paper (see Figure 5-2). Using several responses, demonstrate where the details intersect or are distinctive by writing them in the appropriate section of the Venn diagram.

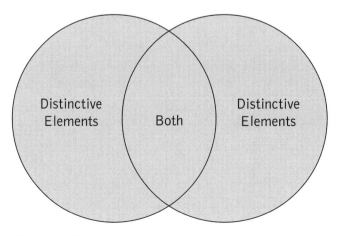

**Figure 5-2.** Venn diagram protocol.

## Postreading Activity

Divide the class into groups of three or four. Provide each group with a hand-out of a Venn diagram copied on 11-inch × 14-inch paper. Using the remaining student responses, select at least 10. Direct each group to write the phrases in the appropriate section of their Venn diagram. When completed, compare Venn diagrams and discuss similarities and differences.

## Independent Practice

The student will take the completed Venn diagram home to share with family members. She will retell the two Cinderella stories with the aid of the Venn diagram and ask which version is preferred. On returning to school, the students will tally Cinderella preferences to select the favorite version.

## Suggested Reading

Climo, S. (1989). *The Egyptian Cinderella*. New York: HarperCollins.
Climo, S. (1993). *The Korean Cinderella*. New York: HarperCollins.

## Notes

## Domain and Area of Instruction

**C**omprehension and strategic reading for narrative text:
Recreational reading
Literacy stage: Basic literacy

### Intended Learning Outcome

With a peer, the student will listen to one audio book per month. After listening, they will discuss the story elements—theme, plot, characters, style, and setting—to the readers' satisfaction.

### Materials

- Tape recorder
- Audio books
- Weekly listening schedule
- Paper and writing instruments

### Prereading Activity

Ask the student to select a listening partner. Next, request them to select one audio book and create a weekly listening schedule (see Figure 5-5). Demonstrate how to note dates, times, and places on the schedule.

### Reading Activity

Using the schedule, the students will listen to the audio book.

### Postreading Activity

Together, the pair will discuss the story elements—theme, plot, characters, style, and setting—and their reactions.

### Independent Practice

The student will select and listen to an audio book alone. He will summarize the content to a willing listener: family member, friend, or rest home resident.

Name _____

| Time | Monday | Tuesday | Wednesday | Thursday | Friday | Saturday | Sunday |
|------|--------|---------|-----------|----------|--------|----------|--------|
| 6–7 | | | | | | | |
| 7–8 | | | | | | | |
| 8–9 | | | | | | | |
| 9–10 | | | | | | | |
| 10–11 | | | | | | | |
| 11–12 | | | | | | | |
| 12–1 | | | | | | | |
| 1–2 | | | | | | | |
| 2–3 | | | | | | | |
| 3–4 | | | | | | | |
| 4–5 | | | | | | | |
| 5–6 | | | | | | | |
| 6–7 | | | | | | | |
| 7–8 | | | | | | | |
| 8–9 | | | | | | | |
| 9–10 | | | | | | | |
| 10–11 | | | | | | | |

**Figure 5-5.**    Weekly listening schedule.

## Notes

_____

_____

_____

_____

_____

_____

## Domain and Area of Instruction

Comprehension and strategic reading for narrative text:
Main ideas and supporting details
Literacy stage: Basic literacy

### Intended Learning Outcome

Given a factual newspaper article that contains quantitative data, the students, working collaboratively, will record the data in the form of a graphic illustration, such as a bar graph, circle graph, or line graph, that represents the main idea and supporting details to the teacher's satisfaction.

### Materials

- Current newspapers
- Paper and writing instruments

### Prereading Activity

Choose a short, interesting newspaper article that contains quantitative information. Introduce it to the class and read it aloud. List the following questions on the board:

1. Who was involved in this event?
2. What took place?
3. Where did it take place?
4. When did it take place?
5. How or why did it take place?

Reread the article and record student responses to the questions on the board. Discuss the details. Explain that details support the main idea and that the main idea is the theme or most important information about the topic. Note that the main idea is often the title of the article. Brainstorm alternate titles.

Show examples of graphic representations: circle graphs, line graphs, bar graphs, and picture graphs. Relate these to the newspaper article by applying the quantitative data to the respective graphic representation.

## Reading Activity

Divide the class into groups of four. Assign each group to choose and read two newspaper articles that contain numbers or data.

## Postreading Activity

For each article, instruct the group to make one graphic representation. Allow time for each group to present its graph, noting the main idea and supporting details.

## Independent Practice

The student will assume the role of a newspaper reporter and write an article of her choice. She will also design a graphic representation, if relevant. When she returns to class, the articles will be collected, revised, and printed as a class newspaper.

## Notes

CHAPTER *6*

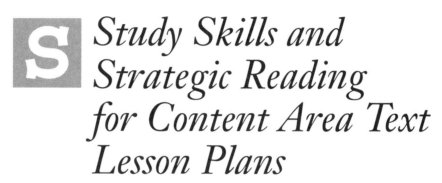

# Study Skills and Strategic Reading for Content Area Text Lesson Plans

## Domain and Area of Instruction

Study skills and strategic reading for content area text: Guide words
Literacy stage: Transitional

### Intended Learning Outcome

Given a list of five words from the dictionary, the student will write the guide words from the page on which each word is located with 90 percent accuracy.

### Materials

- Dictionary
- Guide word worksheets
- Personal dictionaries
- Writing instruments

### Prereading Activity

Distribute sets of guide words from the dictionary and ask questions about the sets: Which word will be found at the bottom of the page? Which word will be first on the page? Will a certain word be found on the page? Provide direct instruction regarding guide words.

### Reading Activity

Give the student two sets of guide words from two dictionary pages and a list of five words. Direct him to write the guide words from the page where each word is located.

### Postreading Activity

In groups of three, have the students compare answers and devise a mutual list. Then, provide the answers. Allow time for discussion.

### Independent Practice

Using a dictionary as a resource, the student will write the guide words for the words in his personal dictionary. On returning to class, the group members will exchange personal dictionaries and evaluate the responses.

### Notes

# Domain and Area of Instruction

S tudy skills and strategic reading for content area text:
    Assessing preknowledge and postknowledge
Literacy stage: Transitional

## Intended Learning Outcome

After instruction, the student will write 8–10 new facts in the "What I learned" section of the K-W-L chart to the teacher's satisfaction.

## Materials

- Live bat in a box
- K-W-L chart (adapted from Ogle, 1986)
- *The Fascinating World of . . . Bats* (Julivert, 1994)
- Writing instruments

## Prereading Activity

Bring to class a live bat in a box. As the students listen to the bat squeak, provide clues as to what is in the box. Once the correct guess is made, show the bat to the class.

Individually, direct each student to complete a K-W-L chart (see Figure 6-1). Instruct them to fill in the K (What I know) section with any facts they *already know* about bats; have them complete the W (What I want to know) section by writing questions regarding what they *want to know* about bats.

## Reading Activity

Assign the students to read silently *The Fascinating World of . . . Bats.*

## Postreading Activity

Have the students complete the K-W-L chart by filling in the L (What I learned) section with 8–10 facts they *learned* about bats from their reading. Arrange the students into groups and provide time for discussion.

## Independent Practice

The student will choose another animal and a relevant, short story. Prior to reading, she will complete the "What I know" and "What I want to know" sections of a K-W-L chart. After reading, she will complete the "What I learned" section. The chart will be submitted for discussion and review.

### Suggested Reading

Julivert, M. A. (1994). *The fascinating world of . . . bats*. New York: Barron's Educational Services.

Name _____

### K-W-L Chart

What I know:



What I want to know:



What I learned:



**Figure 6-1.**   K-W-L chart.

*Source:* Adapted from D. M. Ogle (1986). A teaching model that develops active reading of expository text. *The Reading Teacher, 39,* 564–570. Copyright © 1986 by the International Reading Association. Used by permission of the International Reading Association.

**Notes**

_____

_____

_____

_____

_____

_____

## Domain and Area of Instruction

**S**tudy skills and strategic reading for content area text: Main ideas
Literacy stage: Transitional

### Intended Learning Outcome

After silently reading a newspaper article, the student will answer orally five questions with 80 percent accuracy.

### Materials

- Newspaper
- Written travel directions
- Paper and writing instruments

### Prereading Activity

Read aloud a newspaper article to the student. During the reading, emphasize the main ideas by using intonation. Discuss the importance of main ideas and how they assist in comprehension.

### Reading Activity

Give the student a newspaper to survey. Direct him to select an article to read silently. When he is finished, have him write the main ideas on a piece of paper.

### Postreading Activity

Ask the student the following five questions: Who was involved in this event? What event took place? Where did the event take place? When did the event take place? How or why did the event occur? Direct him to answer the questions by using his notes.

### Independent Practice

Give the student a set of directions describing how to travel from one location to another. Do not reveal the final destination. The student will follow the directions, noting the details. On returning to class, he will state the final destination. Reinforce that the directions are details and that the destination is the main idea.

### Notes

_____

_____

_____

_____

_____

## Domain and Area of Instruction

**S**tudy skills and strategic reading for content area text:
Content-specific vocabulary
Literacy stage: Transitional

### Intended Learning Outcome

For a content area reading assignment, the student will enter unknown words in her personal dictionary, provide the definition for each, and write one original sentence per word, demonstrating knowledge of the word's meaning to the teacher's satisfaction.

### Materials

- Content area textbook
- Construction paper
- Notebook paper
- Stapler

- Multicolored markers
- Writing instruments

## Prereading Activity

Using 26 pieces of notebook paper, one large sheet of construction paper, and a stapler, direct the student to make a personal dictionary. On the top of each page, have her write one letter of the alphabet in alphabetical order. Encourage her to identify and decorate the cover.

## Reading Activity

Assign pages to be read in the content area textbook. While she is reading, instruct her to write unknown words with text page numbers on the appropriate page of her personal dictionary. Encourage her to mentally use context clues, or words surrounding the unknown word, to figure out the word's meaning. Only if she cannot understand the passage should she stop reading and consult a dictionary.

## Postreading Activity

After reading the section, instruct the student to write definitions for all words entered in the personal dictionary. Have her write one original sentence per word that demonstrates knowledge of the word's meaning.

## Independent Practice

Using the words and definitions from her personal dictionary, the student will create a crossword puzzle. On returning to school, the teacher will copy the crossword puzzle and share it with other students.

## Notes

## Domain and Area of Instruction

S tudy skills and strategic reading for content area text:
    Organizational skills
Literacy stage: Transitional

### Intended Learning Outcome

Using a newspaper article, the student will write answers to five questions with 80 percent accuracy.

### Materials

- Newspaper articles
- Board and chalk
- Paper and writing instruments

### Prereading Activity

Choose a short, interesting article from a recent newspaper. Introduce the article to the class and read it aloud. Place the following five questions on the board:

1. Who was involved in this event?
2. What took place?
3. Where did it take place?
4. When did it take place?
5. How or why did it take place?

Ask the students to listen carefully for the answers as you read the article a second time. Elicit answers and write them on the board. Explain that these answers are called supporting details. These lead to the main idea of the article. Point out that the main idea is often similar to the title of the article. Brainstorm additional titles.

### Reading Activity

Divide the class into groups of three or four. Using newspapers, have each group choose an article and read it aloud.

### Postreading Activity

Based on their article, direct each group to write answers to the five questions on the board. Review and discuss.

### Independent Practice

The student will write a news report related to his topic of interest. The report will be edited by his group members and posted on the bulletin board.

### Notes

_____

_____

_____

_____

_____

_____

## Domain and Area of Instruction

**S**tudy skills and strategic reading for content area text: Sequence
Literacy stage: Transitional

### Intended Learning Outcome

After silently reading an article about a famous sportsperson, the student will make a time line sequencing the events in the person's career to the teacher's satisfaction.

### Materials

- *Sports Illustrated for Kids*
- Paper and writing instruments
- Markers
- Construction paper

### Prereading Activity

Discuss what the student knows about the famous sportsperson. Give her a copy of *Sports Illustrated for Kids* that features an article about him. Survey the article for length and possible new terms. Discuss.

### Reading Activity

Direct the student to read the article silently.

### Postreading Activity

Instruct the student to list important dates and events mentioned in the article. Using the markers and construction paper, have her make a time line.

### Independent Practice

The student will display the time line on the Hero Bulletin Board. This is a permanent bulletin board that displays literary heroes or people encountered in print. The displays can be changed periodically, and the class determines the criteria for selection of heroes.

### Suggested Reading

*Sports illustrated for kids.* Birmingham, AL: Time Magazine.

### Notes

_____

_____

_____

_____

_____

## Domain and Area of Instruction

**S**tudy skills and strategic reading for content area text:
   Study skills assessment
Literacy stage: Transitional

### Intended Learning Outcome

The student will write answers to all of the questions on the study skills survey to the teacher's satisfaction.

## Materials

- Board and chalk
- Overhead projector
- Overhead projector pens
- Study skills survey transparency
- Study skills surveys
- Skill sheet for parts of a textbook

## Prereading Activity

Write the following poem on the board:

> Last night I knew the answers.
> Last night I had them pat.
> Last night I could have told you
> Every answer, just like that!
> Last night my brain was cooking.
> Last night I got them right.
> Last night I was a genius.
> So where were you last night! (Harrison, 1992)

Read aloud and discuss interpretations. Lead into the importance of good study skills.

## Reading Activity

Distribute the study skills survey (see Figure 6-2). Have the students answer the questions in writing.

## Postreading Activity

Using the overhead projector and the study skills survey transparency, tally the responses. Read each statement aloud and direct the students to raise their hands to identify the number of *N*s, *S*s, and *U*s. Inform the class that they will be learning new and various ways to improve their study skills.

## Independent Practice

The student will take his study skills survey home and share the results with a family member.

Name _____

## Study Skills Survey

Directions: Write *N* for Never, *S* for Sometimes, and *U* for Usually after the question to describe how often you do the following.  Be honest and thoughtful.

1. Do you look over what you are going to read before you read it?                                   _____

2. Do you form questions about the selection before you read it?                                       _____

3. Do you try to pronounce and define words that are in **bold print** or *italics*?            _____

4. Do you use a slower rate when you are reading a textbook?                                          _____

5. Do you reread the sections that you do not understand?                                              _____

6. Do you outline or take notes as you read?                                                           _____

7. Do you set a time for study?                                                                        _____

8. Do you have a place to study at home or near home?                                                 _____

9. Is the television on when you are studying?                                                         _____

10. Do you review what you have read when you have finished?                                          _____

**Figure 6-2.**    Study skills survey.

## Suggested Reading

Harrison, D. L. (1992). *Somebody catch my homework.* Honesdale, PA: Boyds Mills/Wordsong.

## Notes

_____

_____

_____

## Domain and Area of Instruction

**S**tudy skills and strategic reading for content area text:
    Comprehension monitoring
Literacy stage: Transitional

### Intended Learning Outcome

After selecting a magazine of choice, the student will read three articles and state the main idea for each with 100 percent accuracy.

### Materials

- Student self-selected magazine
- Paper and writing instruments

### Prereading Activity

Direct the student to visit the library and select a magazine. When she returns, ask, "Why did you choose this magazine?" "What articles are of interest?" Have her choose three articles to read.

### Reading Activity

Tell her to read aloud the first article. When she is finished, have her summarize the information and state the main idea.

Next, have her read the second article silently. Likewise, when she is finished, ask her to summarize the article and identify the main idea.

Read aloud the third article to her. When finished, instruct her to retell the information and state the main idea.

### Postreading Activity

Provide 15 minutes for Sustained Silent Reading. Here, the student selects materials and reads for pleasure without interruptions. Have her continue to read the magazine or choose new materials.

### Independent Practice

The student will take the magazine home and continue to read it. When finished, she will return it to the library and choose another.

### Notes

_____

_____

_____

_____

_____

## Domain and Area of Instruction

S tudy skills and strategic reading for content area text: Text organization
Literacy stage: Transitional

### Intended Learning Outcome

After reading aloud a section of *Tide Pools*, the student will orally identify the organizational pattern with 100 percent accuracy.

### Materials

- *Tide Pools* (Rood, 1993)
- Pictures of tide pools
- Starfish and seaweed samples
- Crab and mollusk shells
- Signal words for organizational patterns handouts
- Paper and writing instruments
- White poster board and markers

### Prereading Activity

Ask the students what they already know about tide pools. Invite them to look at the pictures and allow them to examine and discuss the starfish, crab, mollusk, and seaweed samples. Explain that these are found in tide pools.

## Reading Activity

Introduce *Tide Pools* by looking at the cover and discussing the title and picture. Skim through the book, looking at the pictures and reading the table of contents. Then, read aloud the first chapter.

Distribute the signal words for organizational patterns handout (see Figure 6-3). Explain that these words are clues that tell the reader the organizational pattern of the text. If the reader recognizes the organizational pattern, understanding is enhanced.

### Signal Words

The following is a representative list of signal words for the four organizational patterns:

| Sequence | Description | Comparison | Cause-Effect |
|---|---|---|---|
| on | to begin with | however | because |
| not long after | most important | but | since |
| now | also | as well as | therefore |
| as | in fact | on the other hand | consequently |
| before | for instance | not only/but also | as a result |
| after | for example | either . . . or | this led to |
| when | | while | so that |
| first | | although | nevertheless |
| second | | unless | accordingly |
| next | | similarly | if . . . then |
| then | | yet | thus |
| finally | | | |

**Figure 6-3.** Signal words for organizational patterns.

*Source:* Adapted from R. T. Vacca & J. L. Vacca (1999). *Content Area Reading: Literacy and Learning across the Curriculum* (6th ed.). New York: Longman. Copyright © 1999. Reprinted by permission of Addison Wesley Educational Publishing, Inc.

### Postreading Activity

Reread aloud paragraphs that contain signal words. Ask the students to identify the organizational pattern by using their handouts. Discuss.

### Independent Practice

Choosing one organizational pattern, the student will write a paragraph that contains the appropriate signal word(s). When the student returns to class, the paragraphs will be read and discussed.

### Suggested Reading

Rood, R. (1993). *Tide pools.* New York: Harper Trophy.

### Notes

_____

_____

_____

_____

_____

## Domain and Area of Instruction

**S**tudy skills and strategic reading for content area text: Skeleton outline
Literacy stage: Transitional

### Intended Learning Outcome

Using the assigned chapter from the social studies textbook, the student will make a skeleton outline to the teacher's satisfaction.

### Materials

- Social studies textbook
- Board and chalk
- Paper and writing instruments

## Prereading Activity

Explain that knowing the main ideas and supporting details prior to reading enhances understanding. An effective strategy is making a skeleton outline. Here, the reader focuses only on the boldface or larger font headings and sub-headings in the chapter and writes them in outline format. Matching the font size and type is the key to making the outline.

Demonstrate how to make a skeleton outline by using a chapter in the social studies text. The following is a sample outline format:

### CHAPTER TITLE

I. FIRST MAJOR HEADING

II. SECOND MAJOR HEADING
    A. First subheading
    B. Second subheading

III. THIRD MAJOR HEADING
    A. First subheading
    B. Second subheading

## Reading Activity

Assign a chapter in the social studies textbook. Direct the students to read only the chapter headings and subheadings.

## Postreading Activity

Using the chapter headings and subheadings, assign the students to make a skeleton outline.

## Independent Practice

The student will silently read the assigned chapter. He will refer to the skeleton outline to review the main ideas and supporting details.

## Notes

## Domain and Area of Instruction

Study skills and strategic reading for content area text: Location skills
Literacy stage: Basic literacy

### Intended Learning Outcome

When given 10 items and their prices to find in the classified ads section of a Sunday newspaper, the student will scan the ads and list the requested information with 80 percent accuracy.

### Materials

- Classified ads section of a Sunday newspaper
- Paper and writing instruments
- Prepared worksheet with 10 items to locate

### Prereading Activity

Define and discuss the skill of scanning. Scanning is a reading strategy that is used to locate a specific bit of information or a single fact. Together with the student, scan the classified ads section to find five items for sale that might be of use and their respective prices. Examples could include finding a friendly, furry companion, purchasing hay for a horse, or buying a foreign sports car.

### Reading Activity

Give the student a worksheet listing the descriptions of 10 additional items with their costs to be located. Have her use the Sunday classified ads to scan for the information.

### Postreading Activity

Instruct the student to list the items and their prices on the worksheet.

### Independent Practice

The student will ask family members to each name two items that they would like to purchase from the classified ads. Then she will scan the ads and find the items. Finally, she will share the information with the family.

**Notes**

_____

_____

_____

_____

_____

## Domain and Area of Instruction

S tudy skills and strategic reading for content area text: Outlining
Literacy stage: Basic literacy

### Intended Learning Outcome

Given the chapter on Mayans in his social studies textbook, the student will
write answers to six basic questions—who, what, where, when, how, and why—
on a herringbone outline worksheet with 85 percent accuracy.

### Materials

- Social studies textbook
- Tortillas
- *The Mysterious Maya* (Stuart & Stuart, 1977)
- Overhead projector and screen
- Overlay of herringbone outline
- Herringbone outline worksheets (adapted from Gipe, 1998)
- Writing instruments

### Prereading Activity

Distribute tortillas to the students and emphasize that tortillas are food of the
Mayans. Sample the food. Next, show pictures of artifacts and pyramids from
*The Mysterious Maya*.

### Reading Activity

Using an overhead projector displaying a completed herringbone outline (see Figure 6-4), explain how the outline was filled in. Reinforce that the main idea is written on the horizontal line. The answers to the questions are written on the diagonal lines.

Distribute a blank herringbone outline worksheet to the students. Group students into pairs and have them read the first section of the chapter. Direct them to record on the worksheet answers to the questions: Who is being described? When did they live? Where did they live? What did they do? Why did they disappear? How are they remembered? When finished, review and discuss.

### Postreading Activity

Assign the students to read the remainder of the chapter on Mayans. Using information from the chapter, have them continue to add information to the herringbone outline.

### Independent Practice

Using the information on the herringbone outline, the student will describe the Mayans to his parents. Working together, they will write at least two paragraphs describing the Mayans.

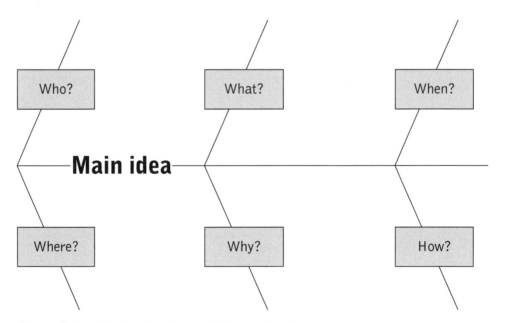

**Figure 6-4.**   The herringbone outline protocol.

*Source:* Adapted with permission from *Multiple Paths to Literacy 4/e* by Joan P. Gipe. Copyright © 1998. Reprinted by permission of Prentice-Hall, Inc., Upper Saddle River, NJ.

### Suggested Reading

Gipe, J. P. (1998). *Multiple paths to literacy: Corrective techniques for classroom teachers* (4th ed.). Upper Saddle River, NJ: Prentice-Hall.

Stuart, G. E., & Stuart, G. S. (1977). *The mysterious Maya*. Washington, DC: National Geographic Society.

### Notes

_____

_____

_____

_____

_____

## Domain and Area of Instruction

Study skills and strategic reading for content area text: Outlining
Literacy stage: Basic literacy

### Intended Learning Outcome

Following group instruction and practice in classifying words, phrases, and sentences, the student will select the main ideas and supporting details of a passage in the science textbook and make an outline with 100 percent accuracy.

### Materials

- Science textbook
- Copies of illustration
- Paper and writing instruments

### Prereading Activity

Write superordinate (general or main idea), subordinate (specific or supporting details), and equal status (equally general or equally specific) words from a passage in the science text on the board. Assist the students in categorizing and classifying the words. Next, demonstrate how to place them in outline format.

## Reading Activity

Assign cooperative groups of students to read a section in their science texts and identify the main ideas and supporting details.

## Postreading Activity

Direct the groups to place the information in outline format. Review and discuss.

In preparation for independent practice, ask the class to select an illustration from the science text that portrays the main ideas and supporting details of the passage. Make copies of the photo.

## Independent Practice

Using a copy of the photo, the student will write one sentence that explains the main idea of the picture. Family members will assist in writing the details. On returning to school, the student will compare her description with those of her peers.

## Notes

## Domain and Area of Instruction

Study skills and strategic reading for content area text: Strategic reading
Literacy stage: Basic literacy

### Intended Learning Outcome

Using a K-W-L chart, the student will write at least three entries regarding what he already knows, what he wants to know, and what he has learned, based on a social studies reading assignment.

### Materials

- Social studies textbook
- K-W-L charts (adapted from Ogle, 1986)
- Writing instruments

### Prereading Activity

Distribute K-W-L charts, and then introduce the chapter to the class. After they look at the title, the pictures and illustrations, and the study outline, provide five minutes for students to write down what they already know *(K)* about the topic on their K-W-L charts (see Figure 6-5). Encourage them to share their notations.

### Reading Activity

Direct the students to write what they would like to know *(W)* about the chapter next. Assign them to silently read the assignment.

### Postreading Activity

When they are finished, have the students complete the "What I learned" *(L)* section. Ask if there are any "What I want to know" questions that were not answered by reading the assignment. Discuss unanswered questions.

### Independent Practice

The student will read the next chapter in the textbook. Given another K-W-L chart, he will complete it.

### Notes

_____

_____

_____

_____

Name _____

## K-W-L Chart

_____

What I know:




_____

What I want to know:




_____

What I learned:




_____

**Figure 6-5.**   K-W-L chart.

*Source:* Adapted from D. M. Ogle (1986). A teaching model that develops active reading of expository text. *The Reading Teacher, 39,* 564–570. Copyright © 1986 by the International Reading Association. Used by permission of the International Reading Association.

## Domain and Area of Instruction

**S**tudy skills and strategic reading for content area text: Fitness
Literacy stage: Basic literacy

### Intended Learning Outcome

For one month, the student will engage in a 30-minute exercise routine three times per week and maintain an exercise journal to the teacher's satisfaction.

### Materials

- Motivating video involving exercise
- Paper and writing instruments
- Exercise journal

### Motivation Activity

Discuss the benefits of exercise. Next, to reinforce the benefits, have the students view a motivating video about exercise. Have the student write a list of the exercises she finds interesting. Discuss the list.

### Exercise Activity

Direct the student to design an exercise routine in which she will engage for one month. Have her maintain an exercise journal to record when and how long she exercised.

### Cool-Down Activity

After one month, review the results of the exercise program.

### Independent Practice

The student will continue her exercise program, working out at least three times a week. She will note progress and changes in attitude and health in her exercise journal.

### Notes

## Domain and Area of Instruction

**S**tudy skills and strategic reading for content area text:
Organizational skills
Literacy stage: Basic literacy

### Intended Learning Outcome

Given a chapter in a content area textbook, the student will recite the main ideas and supporting details of the chapter with 80 percent accuracy.

### Materials

- Content area textbook
- Paper and writing instruments

### Prereading Activity

Introduce the student to the SQ3R (Survey, Question, Read, Recite, Review) study method (Robinson, 1961). In the *survey* step, the student thumbs through the book and chapter noting the illustrations and reading the titles, introductory statements, main headings, and the chapter summary. In the *question* step, the student turns the chapter headings and subheadings into questions and formulates additional questions sparked by surveying. In the *read* step, the student reads each section of the chapter and answers the questions formed in the previous stage. In the *recite* step, the student orally retells the main ideas and supporting details. In the *review* stage, the student reviews the entire chapter by discussing the main ideas and supporting details periodically.

Using the specified textbook and chapter, assign the student to survey the material and create a semantic map or outline of the main ideas and supporting details. Also, request the student to formulate questions about the material.

### Reading Activity

Direct the student to silently read the chapter, keeping in mind the questions asked in the prereading activity, and adjusting his reading speed to accommodate the difficulty of the textbook.

### Postreading Activity

On completion of the reading, have the student fill in the details on the semantic map or outline by using the information in the chapter. Using oral recitation, remind him to periodically review the semantic map or outline at least three times per week.

### Independent Practice

The student will use the SQ3R study method to read and retain information in future textbook chapters.

### Suggested Reading

Robinson, F. P. (1961). *Effective study* (Rev. ed.). New York: Harper & Brothers.

### Notes

_____

_____

_____

_____

_____

_____

## Domain and Area of Instruction

Study skills and strategic reading for content area text: Time management
Literacy stage: Basic literacy

### Intended Learning Outcome

The student will complete and use a weekly schedule during summer vacation to manage her time.

### Materials

- Weekly schedules
- Writing instruments

### Prewriting Activity

Prior to summer vacation, explain to the student the benefits of using time schedules. For example, a schedule provides greater control, encourages balance between work and relaxation, saves time, provides freedom, and increases flexibility.

Model how to complete a weekly schedule (see Figure 6-6). For each day of the week, fill in the time slots, labeling jobs and regularly scheduled activities. Second, fill in life maintenance needs, such as eating and sleeping, and other activities, such as commuting time and household chores. Divide the remaining time between recreation and other summer events.

### Writing Activity

Using the weekly schedule, have the student devise a precise schedule for the first week of summer break. Remind her to account for the following: work, exercise, gardening, social time with friends and family, reading, and viewing television.

### Postwriting Activity

Review the weekly schedule. Probe to discover if any activities were omitted. Encourage her to use the schedule.

### Independent Practice

The student will try out the weekly schedule. Weekly, she will modify the original to accommodate new activities.

### Notes

Name _____

| Time | Monday | Tuesday | Wednesday | Thursday | Friday | Saturday | Sunday |
|---|---|---|---|---|---|---|---|
| 6–7 | | | | | | | |
| 7–8 | | | | | | | |
| 8–9 | | | | | | | |
| 9–10 | | | | | | | |
| 10–11 | | | | | | | |
| 11–12 | | | | | | | |
| 12–1 | | | | | | | |
| 1–2 | | | | | | | |
| 2–3 | | | | | | | |
| 3–4 | | | | | | | |
| 4–5 | | | | | | | |
| 5–6 | | | | | | | |
| 6–7 | | | | | | | |
| 7–8 | | | | | | | |
| 8–9 | | | | | | | |
| 9–10 | | | | | | | |
| 10–11 | | | | | | | |

**Figure 6-6.**    Weekly schedule.

## Domain and Area of Instruction

Study skills and strategic reading for content area text:
Comprehension monitoring
Literacy stage: Basic literacy

### Intended Learning Outcome

Using the ReQuest Procedure (Manzo, 1969), the student will orally answer his partner's questions with 80 percent accuracy.

## Materials

- Magazines that match the reader's interests

## Prereading Activity

Review the ReQuest Procedure. Here, two readers generate questions for their partners to answer. They begin by reading aloud several paragraphs from a selection. One student asks questions, and the partner attempts to answer them without referring to the text. Next, the roles are reversed. After reading additional paragraphs, the partner questions the student. Prior to reading the remainder of the selection, predictions are made. The readers silently read to the end of the piece and compare their predictions to the actual ending.

## Reading Activity

Direct the student to choose a magazine article of his choice. Using the ReQuest Procedure, read it together.

## Postreading Activity

After reading the article, ask the student five questions based on the article's main idea and supporting details. Assess. Discuss the merits of the strategy.

## Independent Practice

Using reading materials of his choice, the student will teach one of his family members the ReQuest Procedure. On returning to class, he will summarize the experience.

## Suggested Reading

Manzo, A. V. (1969). The ReQuest Procedure. *Journal of Reading, 13,* 123–126.

## Notes

## Domain and Area of Instruction

S tudy skills and strategic reading for content area text: Scanning
Literacy stage: Basic literacy

### Intended Learning Outcome

After silently reading a chapter in a textbook, the student will write answers to five completion questions with 100 percent accuracy.

### Materials

- Content area textbook
- Board and chalk
- Completion quiz
- Writing instruments

### Prereading Activity

Scan the assigned chapter for the chapter title, major headings, and subheadings. List them on the board.

Scanning is fast reading to obtain answers to specific questions. It reinforces flexibility in rate of reading, a skill that every reader can and should practice.

### Reading Activity

Direct the student to read the chapter silently.

### Postreading Activity

Based on the chapter headings and subheadings, prepare a five-question completion quiz. Have her take the quiz and fill in the missing terms. Evaluate and discuss.

### Independent Practice

Prior to reading the next chapter in the textbook, the student will scan for the title, headings, and subheadings. On returning to school, she will report on the effectiveness of scanning.

**Notes**

_____

_____

_____

_____

_____

_____

# Domain and Area of Instruction

**S**tudy skills and strategic reading for content area text:
  Organizational skills
Literacy stage: Basic literacy

### Intended Learning Outcome

Given a chapter in a content area textbook, the student will answer from memory two self-generated essay questions with 80 percent accuracy.

### Materials

- Content area textbook
- Two-question essay pop quiz
- Magazine article
- Checklist (teacher made)
- Paper and writing instruments

### Prewriting Activity

Administer an unannounced essay quiz consisting of two questions based on previously read chapter content. Assess. Discuss strategies used to answer the questions and those that should have been used to score higher.

Introduce PORPE (Simpson, 1986), a strategy that stands for _Predict, Organize, Rehearse, Practice,_ and _Evaluate._ The strategy uses writing as the main learning tool for planning, monitoring, and evaluating the reading of content area material.

## Writing Activity

Using the textbook chapter, collaboratively begin the PORPE strategy. First, the student uses the main ideas from the chapter to *predict* and formulate two essay questions. Next, he summarizes and synthesizes the pertinent information in the chapter by *organizing* it into a chart, semantic map, or outline. To place the overall structure and key ideas into long-term memory, he *rehearses* the material aloud and then writes it down. He *practices* by writing responses to the two predicted essay questions from memory.

## Postwriting Activity

*Evaluate* with the student the content and completeness of the two essay responses.

## Independent Practice

The student will use the PORPE strategy to prepare for the next test. Test results will be an indicator of its effectiveness.

## Suggested Reading

Simpson, M. L. (1986). PORPE: A writing strategy for studying and learning in the content areas. *Journal of Reading, 29,* 407–414.

## Notes

## Domain and Area of Instruction

S tudy skills and strategic reading for content area text:
    Comprehension monitoring
Literacy stage: Basic literacy

### Intended Learning Outcome

Choosing and reading an article from a weekly news magazine, the student will write at least five entries for the three categories of the K-W-L chart.

### Materials

- Selection of weekly news magazines
- K-W-L chart (adapted from Ogle, 1986)
- Writing instruments

### Prereading Activity

Survey with the student several weekly news magazines. Request her to choose one magazine and then select an article to read. Inquire as to what she already knows about the article. Working together, complete the "What I know" and "What I want to know" sections of the K-W-L chart (see Figure 6-7). Five entries are required for each category.

### Reading Activity

Have her silently read the magazine article.

### Postreading Activity

Direct the student to complete the "What I learned" section of the K-W-L chart independently. When she is finished, discuss the findings.

### Independent Practice

The student will apply the K-W-L chart to future readings. First, she will list what she already knows about the topic. Second, she will list what she would like to know. Third, after reading the article, she will record what she learned.

### Notes

_____

_____

_____

Name _____

## K-W-L Chart

What I know:

What I want to know:

What I learned:

**Figure 6-7.**   K-W-L chart.

*Source:* Adapted from D. M. Ogle (1986). A teaching model that develops active reading of expository text. *The Reading Teacher, 39,* 564–570. Copyright © 1986 by the International Reading Association. Used by permission of the International Reading Association.

# Domain and Area of Instruction

S tudy skills and strategic reading for content area text:
    Attitude toward reading
Literacy stage: Basic literacy

## Intended Learning Outcome

Given a prereading and postreading attitude survey, the student will score higher on the posttest.

## Materials

- Reading attitude survey
- Reader response journal
- Writing instruments

## Prereading Activity

As a pretest, administer the reading attitude survey (see Figure 6-8). Score the pretest and share the results. If the results are neutral or negative, talk about possible rewards for reading. Next, develop a hierarchy of rewards and the amount of reading necessary to earn a specific reward.

Discuss how reading is a psychological or affective process. A person's self-concept, attitudes in general, attitudes toward reading, interests, and motivation affect the reading process.

## Reading Activity

Based on his interests, direct the student to select books to read for recreation.

## Postreading Activity

Have the student write the books' titles and his reactions in a reader response journal. Review the entries. When he reaches the criteria to earn a reward, celebrate.

After four weeks, administer the reading attitude survey as a posttest. Compare scores and plan accordingly.

## Independent Practice

The student will continue to read for recreation and maintain the reader response journal.

Name _____

Directions: This survey measures how you feel about reading. Read each statement, decide how you feel, and rate each statement on a scale from 1 to 5, as follows:

5 means "I strongly agree."
4 means "I agree."
3 means "I cannot decide."
2 means "I disagree."
1 means "I strongly disagree."

Indicate your feeling by putting X in the proper box. Please be honest. Your responses will not affect your grade in this class.

| | 5 | 4 | 3 | 2 | 1 |
|---|---|---|---|---|---|
| 1. Library books are boring. | | | | | |
| 2. Buying books is a waste of money. | | | | | |
| 3. Reading is one of my hobbies. | | | | | |
| 4. Reading is not enjoyable. | | | | | |
| 5. I am a poor reader. | | | | | |
| 6. I like to read before I go to bed. | | | | | |
| 7. I usually do not finish reading a book. | | | | | |
| 8. Reading gets boring after about 15 minutes. | | | | | |
| 9. Teachers want me to read too much. | | | | | |
| 10. I would like to belong to a book club. | | | | | |
| 11. I don't have enough time to read books. | | | | | |
| 12. You can't learn much from reading. | | | | | |
| 13. I like to have time to read in class. | | | | | |
| 14. Books are good presents. | | | | | |
| 15. I am a poor reader. | | | | | |

Total _____

Scoring: The positive statements are 3, 6, 10, 13, and 14. Total the points as given: 5 = 5, 4 = 4, 3 = 3, 2 = 2, and 1 = 1. The negative items are 1, 2, 4, 5, 7, 8, 9, 11, 12, and 15. Give the opposite number and then score: 5 = 1, 4 = 2, 3 = 3, 2 = 4, and 1 = 5. Scores can range from 15 to 75. A score of 45 represents a neutral attitude toward reading; scores above 45 are more positive; scores below 45 are more negative.

**Figure 6-8.** Reading attitude survey.

**Notes**

_____

_____

_____

_____

_____

_____

# DOMAIN AND AREA OF INSTRUCTION

**S**tudy skills and strategic reading for content area text:
Comprehension monitoring
Literacy stage: Basic literacy

## Intended Learning Outcome

Using a variety of resources, the student will write a biopoem about a famous individual to the teacher's satisfaction.

## Materials

- Documentary video on selected famous individual
- Social studies textbook
- Resources on selected famous individual
- Paper and drawing materials

## Prereading Activity

View a documentary video about the famous individual. Host a "Say What I Saw." The students will each draw an event from the video and then give the picture to the person on their left side. This person, without showing the picture to the group, will describe it and "say what the other person saw" while viewing the video.

## Reading Activity

Using the social studies textbook, assign the student to read silently the section on the selected famous individual. To augment this information, have her visit the library for additional resources.

## Postreading Activity

Direct the student to write a biopoem about the person. A biopoem is an unrhymed form comprised of 11 lines that are not written in complete sentences. Words such as *I, me,* and *my* are not used. Each line begins with certain words or traits and presents specified information as follows (Gere, 1985):

Line  1   First name of subject
Line  2   Four traits that describe the subject
Line  3   Tell who is a relative of the subject
Line  4   Tell what the subject cares about (3 items)
Line  5   Tell what the subject is feeling (3 items)
Line  6   Tell about things the subject needs (3 items)
Line  7   Tell what the subject fears (3 items)
Line  8   Tell what the subject gives (3 items)
Line  9   Tell what the subject would like to see (3 items)
Line 10   Tell where the subject lived
Line 11   Last name

Share and display.

## Independent Practice

The student will share her biopoem with family members or friends. She will use this format to explore additional historical persons.

## Suggested Reading

Gere, A. R. (1985). *Roots in the sawdust: Writing to learn across the disciplines.* Urbana, IL: National Council of Teachers of English.

## Notes

## Domain and Area of Instruction

Study skills and strategic reading for content area text:
Content-specific vocabulary
Literacy stage: Basic literacy

### Intended Learning Outcome

Given 20 vocabulary words from the story "A River Runs through It," the student will write a summary by using the words in context with 100 percent accuracy.

### Materials

- *A River Runs through It and Other Stories* (Maclean, 1976)
- *A River Runs through It* (1992) videotape
- Handout with 20 teacher-selected words from "A River Runs through It"
- Dictionary
- Paper and writing instruments

### Prereading Activity

View segments of the video *A River Runs through It*. Discuss the setting. Then, arrange a field trip to the nearest river or body of water. Invite a local expert to introduce the art of fly-fishing.

Give the student the handout with 20 teacher-selected vocabulary words from "A River Runs through It." Preview them.

### Reading Activity

Assign him to silently read the story. Direct him to write the entire sentence on the handout as he encounters the 20 vocabulary words.

### Postreading Activity

Using context clues and/or the dictionary, have the student define each term. Assign him to write a summary of the story that uses the 20 words. Read and discuss.

### Independent Practice

The student will take a friend or family member to a river or other body of water. He will use the vocabulary words to describe the story and fly-fishing.

### Suggested Reading

Maclean, N. (1976). *A river runs through it and other stories.* New York: Pocket Books.

Redford, R. (Director). (1992). *A river runs through it* [Videotape]. (Available from Columbia TriStar Home Video, Los Angeles, CA)

### Notes

_____

_____

_____

_____

_____

## Domain and Area of Instruction

**S**tudy skills and strategic reading for content area text:
    Main ideas and supporting details
Literacy stage: Basic literacy

### Intended Learning Outcome

Given a short story of interest to the student, she will outline the main ideas and supporting details with 90 percent accuracy.

### Materials

- Short stories
- Board and chalk
- Paper
- Writing instruments
- Incomplete outlines

### Prereading Activity

Read aloud a short story. Discuss the story line and determine the main ideas and supporting details. Demonstrate how to use these to make an outline.

### Reading Activity

Give the student a list of five short stories. Have her select one story to read silently.

### Postreading Activity

Give the student an incomplete outline of the main ideas and supporting details of the story. For example, the details are listed, but the main idea line is blank. Instruct her to complete the outline. Review and discuss.

### Independent Practice

The student will choose one television show to watch and outline. The outline will include the main ideas and supporting details. On returning to school, the student will present her outline.

### Notes

_____

_____

_____

_____

_____

_____

# *Literacy Lesson Plan Template*

**Domain and Area of Instruction**

_____

_____

**Intended Learning Outcome**

_____

_____

**Materials**

_____

_____

**Prereading Activity**

_____

_____

**Reading Activity**

_____

_____

**Postreading Activity**

_____

_____

**Independent Practice**

_____

_____

**Suggested Reading and/or Notes**

_____

_____

APPENDIX **B**

# *National Awards for Children's Literature*

## THE CALDECOTT MEDAL

Named in honor of nineteenth-century English illustrator Randolph Caldecott, the Caldecott Medal is awarded annually by the Association for Library Service to Children, a division of the American Library Association, to the artist of the most distinguished American picture book for children. Honor books are also recognized. The following lists the award winner in capital letters; the honor books are italicized.

1938 ANIMALS OF THE BIBLE: A PICTURE BOOK. Text selected
from the King James Bible, by H. D. Fish. Illustrated by
D. P. Lathrop. Lippincott.
*Seven Simeons*, by B. Artzybasheff. Viking.
*Four and Twenty Blackbirds*, compiled by H. D. Fish. Illustrated by
R. Lawson. Stokes.

1939 MEI LI, by T. Handforth. Doubleday.
*The Forest Pool*, by L. A. Armer. Longmans.
*Wee Gillis*, by M. Leaf. Illustrated by R. Lawson. Viking.
*Snow White and the Seven Dwarfs*, translated and illustrated by
W. Gág. Coward.
*Barkis*, by C. T. Newberry. Harper.
*Andy and the Lion*, by J. Daugherty. Viking.

1940    ABRAHAM LINCOLN, by I. d'Aulaire and E. P. d'Aulaire.
        Doubleday.
        *Cock-a-Doodle-Doo*, by B. Hader and E. Hader. Macmillan.
        *Madeline*, by L. Bemelmans. Viking.
        *The Ageless Story*, by L. Ford. Dodd.

1941    THEY WERE STRONG AND GOOD, by R. Lawson. Viking.
        *April's Kittens*, by C. T. Newberry. Harper.

1942    MAKE WAY FOR DUCKLINGS, by R. McCloskey. Viking.
        *An American ABC*, by M. Petersham and M. Petersham. Macmillan.
        *In My Mother's House*, by A. N. Clark. Illustrated by V. Gerrera. Viking.
        *Paddle-to-the-Sea*, by H. C. Holling. Houghton.
        *Nothing at All*, by W. Gág. Coward-McCann.

1943    THE LITTLE HOUSE, by V. L. Burton. Houghton.
        *Dash and Dart*, by M. Buff and C. Buff. Viking.
        *Marshmallow*, by C. T. Newberry. Harper.

1944    MANY MOONS, by J. Thurber. Illustrated by L. Slobodkin. Harcourt.
        *Small Rain*. Text arranged from the Bible by J. O. Jones. Illustrated by
        E. O. Jones. Viking.
        *Pierre Pigeon*, by L. Kingman. Illustrated by A. E. Bare. Houghton.
        *Good-Luck Horse*, by C. Chan. Illustrated by P. Chan. Whittlesey.
        *Mighty Hunter*, by B. Hader and E. Hader. Macmillan.
        *A Child's Good Night Book*, by M. W. Brown. Illustrated by J. Charlot.
        Scott.

1945    PRAYER FOR A CHILD, by R. Field. Pictures by E. O. Jones.
        Macmillan.
        *Mother Goose*. Compiled and illustrated by T. Tudor. Walck.
        *In the Forest*, by M. H. Ets. Viking.
        *Yonie Wondernose*, by M. de Angeli. Doubleday.
        *The Christmas Anna Angel*, by R. Sawyer. Illustrated by K. Seredy.
        Viking.

1946    THE ROOSTER CROWS . . . (traditional Mother Goose).
        Illustrated by M. Petersham and M. Petersham. Macmillan.
        *Little Lost Lamb*, by G. MacDonald. Illustrated by L. Weisgard.
        Doubleday.
        *Sing Mother Goose*. Music by O. Wheeler. Illustrated by M. Torrey.
        Dutton.
        *My Mother Is the Most Beautiful Woman in the World*, by B. Reyher.
        Illustrated by R. C. Gannett. Lothrop.
        *You Can Write Chinese*, by K. Wiese. Viking.

1947    THE LITTLE ISLAND, by G. MacDonald. Illustrated by
           L. Weisgard. Doubleday.
       *Rain Drop Splash*, by A. R. Tresselt. Illustrated by L. Weisgard.
           Lothrop.
       *Boats on the River*, by M. Flack. Illustrated by J. H. Barnum. Viking.
       *Timothy Turtle*, by A. Graham. Illustrated by T. Palazzo. Viking.
       *Pedro, the Angel of Olvera Street*, by L. Politi. Scribner's.
       *Sing in Praise*, by O. Wheeler. Illustrated by M. Torrey. Dutton.

1948    WHITE SNOW, BRIGHT SNOW, by A. Tresselt. Illustrated by
           R. Duvoisin. Lothrop.
       *Stone Soup.* Told and illustrated by M. Brown. Scribner's.
       *McElligot's Pool*, by T. S. Geisel (Dr. Seuss). Random.
       *Bambino the Clown*, by G. Schreiber. Viking.
       *Roger and the Fox*, by L. R. Davis. Illustrated by H. Woodward.
           Doubleday.
       *Song of Robin Hood*, A. Malcolmson, ed. Illustrated by V. L. Burton.
           Houghton.

1949    THE BIG SNOW, by B. Hader and E. Hader. Macmillan.
       *Blueberries for Sal*, by R. McCloskey. Viking.
       *All Around the Town*, by P. McGinley. Illustrated by H. Stone.
           Lippincott.
       *Juanita*, by L. Politi. Scribner's.
       *Fish in the Air*, by K. Wiese. Viking.

1950    SONG OF THE SWALLOWS, by L. Politi. Scribner's.
       *America's Ethan Allen*, by S. Holbrook. Illustrated by L. Ward.
           Houghton.
       *The Wild Birthday Cake*, by L. R. Davis. Illustrated by H. Woodward.
           Doubleday.
       *Happy Day*, by R. Krauss. Illustrated by M. Simont. Harper.
       *Henry Fisherman*, by M. Brown. Scribner's.
       *Bartholomew and the Oobleck*, by T. S. Geisel (Dr. Seuss). Random.

1951    THE EGG TREE, by K. Milhous. Scribner's.
       *Dick Whittington and His Cat*, told and illustrated by M. Brown.
           Scribner's.
       *The Two Reds*, by Will (W. Lipkind). Illustrated by Nicolas
           (Mordvinoff). Harcourt.
       *If I Ran the Zoo*, by T. S. Geisel (Dr. Seuss). Random.
       *T-Bone, the Baby-Sitter*, by C. T. Newberry. Harper.
       *The Most Wonderful Doll in the World*, by P. McGinley. Illustrated by
           H. Stone. Lippincott.

1952    FINDERS KEEPERS, by Will (W. Lipkind). Illustrated by Nicolas (Mordvinoff). Harcourt.
*Mr. T. W. Anthony Woo*, by M. H. Ets. Viking.
*Skipper John's Cook*, by M. Brown. Scribner's.
*All Falling Down*, by G. Zion. Illustrated by M. B. Graham. Harper.
*Bear Party*, by W. Pène du Bois. Viking.
*Feather Mountain*, by E. Olds. Houghton.

1953    THE BIGGEST BEAR, by L. Ward. Houghton.
*Puss in Boots.* Told and illustrated by M. Brown. Scribner's.
*One Morning in Maine*, by R. McCloskey. Viking.
*Ape in a Cape*, by F. Eichenberg. Harcourt.
*The Storm Book*, by C. Zolotow. Illustrated by M. B. Graham. Harper.
*Five Little Monkeys*, by J. Kepes. Houghton.

1954    MADELINE'S RESCUE, by L. Bemelmans. Viking.
*Journey Cake, Ho!* by R. Sawyer. Illustrated by R. McCloskey. Viking.
*When Will the World Be Mine?* by M. Schlein. Illustrated by J. Charlot. Scott.
*The Steadfast Tin Soldier*, translated by M. R. James. Adapted from Hans Christian Andersen. Illustrated by M. Brown. Scribner's.
*A Very Special House*, by R. Krauss. Illustrated by M. Sendak. Harper.
*Green Eyes*, by A. Birnbaum. Capitol.

1955    CINDERELLA, by C. Perrault. Illustrated by M. Brown. Scribner's.
*Book of Nursery and Mother Goose Rhymes.* Compiled and illustrated by M. de Angeli. Doubleday.
*Wheel on the Chimney*, by M. W. Brown. Illustrated by T. Gergely. Lippincott.
*The Thanksgiving Story*, by A. Dalgliesh. Illustrated by H. Sewell. Scribner's.

1956    FROG WENT A-COURTIN', by J. Langstaff. Illustrated by F. Rojankovsky. Harcourt.
*Play with Me*, by M. H. Ets. Viking.
*Crow Boy*, by T. Yashima. Viking.

1957    A TREE IS NICE, by J. M. Udry. Illustrated by M. Simont. Harper.
*Mr. Penny's Race Horse*, by M. H. Ets. Viking.
*1 Is One*, by T. Tudor. Walck.
*Anatole*, by E. Titus. Illustrated by P. Galdone. McGraw.
*Gillespie and the Guards*, by B. Elkin. Illustrated by J. Daugherty. Viking.
*Lion*, by W. Pène du Bois. Viking.

1958　TIME OF WONDER, by R. McCloskey. Viking.
*Fly High, Fly Low*, by D. Freeman. Viking.
*Anatole and the Cat*, by E. Titus. Illustrated by P. Galdone. McGraw.

1959　CHANTICLEER AND THE FOX. Edited and illustrated by
　　　　B. Cooney. Crowell.
*The House That Jack Built*, by A. Frasconi. Harcourt.
*What Do You Say, Dear?* by S. Joslin. Illustrated by M. Sendak. Scott.
*Umbrella*, by T. Yashima. Viking.

1960　NINE DAYS TO CHRISTMAS, by M. H. Ets and A. Labastida.
　　　　Viking.
*Houses from the Sea*, by A. E. Goudey. Illustrated by A. Adams.
　　　　Scribner's.
*The Moon Jumpers*, by J. M. Udry. Illustrated by M. Sendak. Harper.

1961　BABOUSHKA AND THE THREE KINGS, by R. Robbins.
　　　　Illustrated by N. Sidjakov. Parnassus.
*Inch by Inch*, by L. Lionni. Obolensky.

1962　ONCE A MOUSE, by M. Brown. Scribner's.
*The Fox Went Out on a Chilly Night*, by P. Spier. Doubleday.
*Little Bear's Visit*, by E. Minarik. Illustrated by M. Sendak. Harper.
*The Day We Saw the Sun Come Up*, by A. Goudey. Illustrated by
　　　　A. Adams. Scribner's.

1963　THE SNOWY DAY, by E. J. Keats. Viking.
*The Sun Is a Golden Earring*, by N. Belting. Illustrated by B. Bryson.
　　　　Holt.
*Mr. Rabbit and the Lovely Present*, by C. Zolotow. Illustrated by
　　　　M. Sendak. Harper.

1964　WHERE THE WILD THINGS ARE, by M. Sendak. Harper.
*Swimmy*, by L. Lionni. Pantheon.
*All in the Morning Early*, by S. N. Leodhas. Illustrated by E. Ness.
　　　　Holt.
*Mother Goose and Nursery Rhymes*, illustrated by P. Reed. Atheneum.

1965　MAY I BRING A FRIEND? by B. Schenk de Regniers. Illustrated by
　　　　B. Montresor. Atheneum.
*Rain Makes Applesauce*, by J. Scheer. Illustrated by M. Bileck. Holiday.
*The Wave*, by M. Hodges. Illustrated by B. Lent. Houghton.
*A Pocketful of Cricket*, by R. Caudill. Illustrated by E. Ness. Holt.

1966    ALWAYS ROOM FOR ONE MORE, by S. N. Leodhas. Illustrated by N. Hogrogian. Holt.
*Hide and Seek Fog*, by A. Tresselt. Illustrated by R. Duvoisin. Lothrop.
*Just Me*, by M. H. Ets. Viking.
*Tom Tit Tot*, J. Jacobs, ed. Illustrated by E. Ness. Scribner's.

1967    SAM, BANGS AND MOONSHINE, by E. Ness. Holt.
*One Wide River to Cross*, by B. Emberley. Illustrated by E. Emberley. Prentice.

1968    DRUMMER HOFF, by B. Emberley. Illustrated by E. Emberley. Prentice.
*Frederick*, by L. Lionni. Pantheon.
*Seashore Story*, by T. Yashima. Viking.
*The Emperor and the Kite*, by J.Yolen. Illustrated by E. Young. World.

1969    THE FOOL OF THE WORLD AND THE FLYING SHIP, by A. Ransome. Illustrated by U. Shulevitz. Farrar, Straus & Giroux.
*Why the Sun and the Moon Live in the Sky*, by E. Dayrell. Illustrated by B. Lent. Houghton.

1970    SYLVESTER AND THE MAGIC PEBBLE, by W. Steig. Windmill.
*Goggles!* by E. J. Keats. Macmillan.
*Alexander and the Wind-Up Mouse*, by L. Lionni. Pantheon.
*Pop Corn and Ma Goodness*, by E. M. Preston. Illustrated by R. A. Parker. Viking.
*Thy Friend, Obadiah*, by B. Turkle. Viking.
*The Judge*, by H. Zemach. Illustrated by M. Zemach. Farrar, Straus & Giroux.

1971    A STORY, A STORY, by G. E. Haley. Atheneum.
*The Angry Moon*, by W. Sleator. Illustrated by B. Lent. Atlantic/Little.
*Frog and Toad Are Friends*, by A. Lobel. Harper.
*In the Night Kitchen*, by M. Sendak. Harper.

1972    ONE FINE DAY, by N. Hogrogian. Macmillan.
*If All the Seas Were One Sea*, by J. Domanska. Macmillan.
*Moja Means One: Swahili Counting Book*, by M. Feelings. Illustrated by T. Feelings. Dial.
*Hildilid's Night*, by C. D. Ryan. Illustrated by A. Lobel. Macmillan.

1973    THE FUNNY LITTLE WOMAN, retold by A. Mosel. Illustrated by B. Lent. Dutton.
*Hosie's Alphabet*, by H. Baskin, T. Baskin, and L. Baskin. Illustrated by L. Baskin. Viking.

*When Clay Sings*, by B. Baylor. Illustrated by T. Bahti. Scribner's.
*Snow-White and the Seven Dwarfs*, by the Brothers Grimm. Translated by R. Jarrell. Illustrated by N. E. Burkert. Farrar, Straus & Giroux.
*Anansi the Spider*, adapted and illustrated by G. McDermott. Holt.

1974    DUFFY AND THE DEVIL, by H. Zemach. Illustrated by M. Zemach. Farrar, Straus & Giroux.
*The Three Jovial Huntsmen*, by S. Jeffers. Bradbury.
*Cathedral*, by D. Macaulay. Houghton.

1975    ARROW TO THE SUN, adapted and illustrated by G. McDermott. Viking.
*Jambo Means Hello: Swahili Alphabet Book*, by M. Feelings. Illustrated by T. Feelings. Dial.

1976    WHY MOSQUITOES BUZZ IN PEOPLE'S EARS, retold by V. Aardema. Illustrated by L. Dillon and D. Dillon. Dial.
*The Desert Is Theirs*, by B. Baylor. Illustrated by P. Parnell. Scribner's.
*Strega Nona*, retold and illustrated by T. de Paola. Prentice.

1977    ASHANTI TO ZULU: AFRICAN TRADITIONS, by M. Musgrove. Illustrated by L. Dillon and D. Dillon. Dial.
*The Amazing Bone*, by W. Steig. Farrar.
*The Contest*, retold and illustrated by N. Hogrogian. Greenwillow.
*Fish for Supper*, by M. B. Goffstein. Dial.
*The Golem*, by B. B. McDermott. Lippincott.
*Hawk, I'm Your Brother*, by B. Baylor. Illustrated by P. Parnall. Scribner's.

1978    NOAH'S ARK, by P. Spier. Doubleday.
*Castle*, by D. Macaulay. Houghton.
*It Could Always Be Worse*, retold and illustrated by M. Zemach. Farrar, Straus & Giroux.

1979    THE GIRL WHO LOVED WILD HORSES, by P. Goble. Bradbury.
*Freight Train*, by D. Crews. Greenwillow.
*The Way to Start a Day*, by B. Baylor. Illustrated by P. Parnall. Scribner's.

1980    OX-CART MAN, by D. Hall. Illustrated by B. Cooney. Viking.
*Ben's Trumpet*, by R. Isadora. Greenwillow.
*The Treasure*, by U. Shulevitz. Farrar.
*The Garden of Abdul Gasazi*, by C. Van Allsburg. Houghton.

1981    FABLES, by A. Lobel. Harper.
       *The Bremen-Town Musicians*, by I. Plume. Doubleday.
       *The Grey Lady and the Strawberry Snatcher*, by M. Bang. Four Winds.
       *Mice Twice*, by J. Low. McElderry/Atheneum.
       *Truck*, by D. Crews. Greenwillow.

1982    JUMANJI, by C. Van Allsburg. Houghton.
       *A Visit to William Blake's Inn: Poems for Innocent and Experienced
          Travelers*, by N. Willard. Illustrated by A. Provensen and
          M. Provensen. Harcourt.
       *Where the Buffaloes Begin*, by O. Baker. Illustrated by S. Gammell.
          Warne.
       *On Market Street*, by A. Lobel. Illustrated by A. Lobel. Greenwillow.
       *Outside Over There*, by M. Sendak. Harper.

1983    SHADOW, by B. Cendrars. Translated and illustrated by M. Brown.
          Scribner's.
       *When I Was Young in the Mountains*, by C. Rylant. Illustrated by
          D. Goode. Dutton.
       *A Chair for My Mother*, by V. B. Williams. Greenwillow.

1984    THE GLORIOUS FLIGHT: ACROSS THE CHANNEL WITH
          LOUIS BLÉRIOT, JULY 25, 1909, by A. Provensen and
          M. Provensen. Viking.
       *Ten, Nine, Eight*, by M. Bang. Greenwillow.
       *Little Red Riding Hood*, retold and illustrated by T. S. Hyman. Holiday.

1985    SAINT GEORGE AND THE DRAGON, adapted by M. Hodges.
          Illustrated by T. S. Hyman. Little, Brown.
       *Hansel and Gretel*, retold by R. Lesser. Illustrated by P. O. Zelinsky.
          Dodd.
       *The Story of Jumping Mouse*, by J. Steptoe. Lothrop.
       *Have You Seen My Duckling?* by N. Tafuri. Greenwillow.

1986    THE POLAR EXPRESS, by C. Van Allsburg. Houghton.
       *The Relatives Came*, by C. Rylant. Illustrated by S. Gammell. Bradbury.
       *King Bidgood's in the Bathtub*, by A. Wood. Illustrated by D. Wood.
          Harcourt.

1987    HEY AL, by A. Yorinks. Illustrated by R. Egielski. Farrar, Straus &
          Giroux.
       *Alphabatics*, by S. MacDonald. Bradbury.
       *Rumpelstiltskin*, adapted and illustrated by P. O. Zelinsky. Dutton.
       *The Village of Round and Square Houses*, by A. Grifalconi. Little, Brown.

1988    OWL MOON, by J. Yolen. Illustrated by J. Schoenherr. Philomel.
*Mufaro's Beautiful Daughters: An African Story*, adapted and illustrated
     by J. Steptoe. Lothrop.

1989    SONG AND DANCE MAN, by K. Ackerman. Illustrated by
     S. Gammell. Knopf.
*The Boy of the Three-Year Nap*, by D. Stanley. Illustrated by A. Say.
     Houghton.
*Free Fall*, by D. Wiesner. Lothrop.
*Goldilocks and the Three Bears*, adapted and illustrated by J. Marshall.
     Dial.
*Mirandy and Brother Wind*, by P. McKissack. Illustrated by J. Pinkney.
     Knopf.

1990    LON PO PO: A RED RIDING HOOD STORY FROM CHINA,
     adapted and illustrated by E. Young. Philomel.
*Bill Peet: An Autobiography*, by B. Peet. Houghton.
*Color Zoo*, by L. Ehlert. Lippincott.
*Herschel and the Hanukkah Goblins*, by E. Kimmel. Illustrated by
     T. S. Hyman. Holiday House.
*The Talking Eggs*, by R. D. San Souci. Illustrated by J. Pinkney. Dial.

1991    BLACK AND WHITE, by D. Macaulay. Houghton.
*Puss in Boots*, by C. Perrault. Translated by M. Arthur. Illustrated by
     F. Marcellino. Farrar, Straus & Giroux.
*"More More More Snow," Said the Baby*, by V. B. Williams. Greenwillow.

1992    TUESDAY, by D. Wiesner. Clarion.
*Tar Beach*, by F. Ringgold. Crown.

1993    MIRETTE ON THE HIGH WIRE, by E. A. McCully. Putnam.
*The Stinky Cheese Man and Other Fairly Stupid Tales*, by J. Scieszka.
     Illustrated by L. Smith. Viking.
*Working Cotton*, by S. A. Williams. Illustrated by C. Byard. Harcourt.
*Seven Blind Mice*, by E. Young. Philomel.

1994    GRANDFATHER'S JOURNEY, by A. Say. Houghton.
*Peppe the Lamplighter*, by E. Bartone. Illustrated by T. Lewin. Lothrop.
*In the Small, Small Pond*, by D. Fleming. Holt.
*Owen*, by K. Henkes. Greenwillow.
*Raven: The Trickster Tale from the Pacific Northwest*, by G. McDermott.
     Harcourt.
*Yo! Yes?* by C. Raschka. Orchard.

1995    SMOKY NIGHT, by E. Bunting. Illustrated by D. Diaz. Harcourt.
        *Swamp Angel*, by A. Isaacs. Illustrated by P. O. Zelinsky. Dutton.
        *John Henry*, by J. Lester. Illustrated by J. Pinkney. Dial.
        *Time Flies*, by E. Rohmann. Crown.

1996    OFFICER BUCKLE AND GLORIA, by P. Rathmann. Putnam.
        *Alphabet City*, by S. T. Johnson. Viking.
        *Zin! Zin! Zin!*, by L. Moss. Illustrated by M. Priceman. Simon &
            Schuster.
        *The Faithful Friend*, by R. D. San Souci. Illustrated by B. Pinkney.
            Simon & Schuster.
        *Tops and Bottoms*, by J. Stevens. Harcourt.

1997    GOLEM, by D. Wisniewski. Clarion.
        *Hush!: A Thai Lullaby*, by M. Ho. Illustrated by H. Meade. Kroupa/
            Orchard.
        *The Graphic Alphabet*. Illustrated by D. Pelletier. Orchard.
        *The Paperboy*, by D. Pilkey. Jackson/Orchard.
        *Starry Messenger*, by P. Sis. Foster/Farrar.

1998    RAPUNZEL, by P. Zelinsky. Dutton.
        *Harlem: A Poem*, by W. D. Myers. Illustrated by C. Myers. Scholastic.
        *The Gardener*, by S. Stewart. Illustrated by D. Small. Farrar, Straus &
            Giroux.
        *There Was an Old Lady Who Swallowed a Fly*, by S. Taback. Viking.

1999    SNOWFLAKE BENTLEY, by J. B. Martin. Illustrated by M. Azarian.
            Houghton Mifflin.
        *Duke Ellington: The Piano Prince and the Orchestra*, by A. D. Pinkney.
            Illustrated by B. Pinkney. Hyperion.
        *No, David!*, by D. Shannon. Blue Sky/Scholastic.
        *Snow*, by U. Shulevitz. Farrar, Straus & Giroux.
        *Tibet: Through the Red Box*, by P. Sis. Farrar, Straus & Giroux.

2000    JOSEPH HAD A LITTLE OVERCOAT, adapted and illustrated by
            S. Taback. Viking
        *Sector 7*, by D. Weisner. Clarion Books.
        *The Ugly Duckling*, adapted and illustrated by J. Pinkney. Morrow.
        *When Sophie Gets Angry—Really, Really Angry*, by M. Bang. Scholastic.
        *A Child's Calendar*, by J. Updike. Illustrated by T. S. Hyman. Holiday
            House.

## THE NEWBERY MEDAL

The Newbery Medal, named for the eighteenth-century British bookseller John Newbery, is awarded annually by the Association for Library Service to Children, a division of the American Library Association, to the author of the most distinguished contribution to American literature for children. Honor books are also recognized. The following lists the award winner in capital letters; the honor books are italicized.

1922   THE STORY OF MANKIND, by H. W. Van Loon. Liveright.
*The Great Quest*, by C. B. Hawes. Little, Brown.
*Cedric the Forester*, by B. G. Marshall. Appleton.
*The Old Tobacco Shop*, by W. Bowen. Macmillan.
*The Golden Fleece*, by P. Colum. Macmillan.
*Windy Hill*, by C. Meigs. Macmillan.

1923   THE VOYAGES OF DOCTOR DOLITTLE, by H. Lofting. Harper.
(No record of honor books)

1924   THE DARK FRIGATE, by C. B. Hawes. Little, Brown.
(No record of honor books)

1925   TALES FROM SILVER LANDS, by C. J. Finger. Illustrated by P. Honore. Doubleday.
*Nicholas*, by A. C. Moore. Putnam.
*Dream Coach*, by A. Parrish and D. Parrish. Macmillan.

1926   SHEN OF THE SEA, by A. B. Chrisman. Illustrated by E. Hasselriis. Dutton.
*The Voyagers*, by P. Colum. Macmillan.

1927   SMOKY, THE COWHORSE, by W. James. Scribner's.
(No record of honor books)

1928   GAY NECK, by D. G. Mukerji. Illustrated by B. Artzybasheff. Dutton.
*The Wonder-Smith and His Son*, by E. Young. Longmans.
*Downright Dencey*, by C. D. Snedeker. Doubleday.

1929   TRUMPETER OF KRAKOW, by E. P. Kelly. Illustrated by A. Pruszynska. Macmillan.
*The Pigtail of Ah Lee Ben Loo*, by J. Bennett. Longmans.
*Millions of Cats*, by W. Gág. Coward-McCann.
*The Boy Who Was*, by G. T. Hallock. Dutton.
*Clearing Weather*, by C. Meigs. Little, Brown.

*The Runaway Papoose*, by G. P. Moon. Doubleday.
*Tod of the Fens*, by E. Whitney. Macmillan.

1930   HITTY, HER FIRST HUNDRED YEARS, by R. Field. Illustrated
by D. P. Lathrop. Macmillan.
*The Tangle-Coated Horse and Other Tales: Episodes from the Fionn Saga*,
by E. Young. Illustrated by V. Brock. Longmans.
*Vaino: A Boy of New Finland*, by J. D. Adams. Illustrated by L. Ostman.
Dutton.
*Pran of Albania*, by E. C. Miller. Doubleday.
*The Jumping-Off Place*, by M. H. McNeely. McKay/Longmans.
*A Daughter of the Seine*, by J. Eaton. Harper.
*Little Blacknose*, by H. H. Swift. Illustrated by L. Ward. Harcourt.

1931   THE CAT WHO WENT TO HEAVEN, by E. Coatsworth.
Illustrated by L. Ward. Macmillan.
*Floating Island*, by A. Parrish. Harper.
*The Dark Star of Itza*, by A. Malkus. Harcourt.
*Queer Person*, by R. Hubbard. Doubleday.
*Mountains Are Free*, by J. D. Adams. Dutton.
*Spice and the Devil's Cave*, by A. D. Hewes. Knopf.
*Meggy McIntosh*, by E. J. Gray. Doubleday.
*Garram the Hunter: A Boy of the Hill Tribes*, by H. Best. Illustrated by
A. Best. Doubleday.
*Ood-Le-Uk, The Wanderer*, by A. Lide and M. Johansen. Illustrated by
R. Lufkin. Little, Brown.

1932   WATERLESS MOUNTAIN, by L. A. Armer. Illustrated by S. Armer
and the author. Longmans.
*The Fairy Circus*, by D. Lathrop. Macmillan.
*Calico Bush*, by R. Field. Macmillan.
*Boy of the South Seas*, by E. Tietjens. Coward-McCann.
*Out of the Flame*, by E. Lounsbery. Longmans.
*Jane's Island*, by M. H. Alee. Houghton.
*Truce of the Wolf*, by M. G. Davis. Harcourt.

1933   YOUNG FU OF THE UPPER YANGTZE, by E. F. Lewis.
Illustrated by K. Wiese. Winston.
*Swift Rivers*, by C. Meigs. Little, Brown.
*The Railroad to Freedom*, by H. Swift. Harcourt.
*Children of the Soil*, by N. Burglon. Doubleday.

1934   INVINCIBLE LOUISA, by C. Meigs. Little, Brown.
*Forgotten Daughter*, by C. D. Snedeker. Doubleday.
*Swords of Steel*, by E. Singmaster. Houghton.
*ABC Bunny*, by W. Gág. Coward-McCann.
*Winged Girl of Knossos*, by E. Berry. Appleton.
*New Land*, by S. L. Schmidt. McBride.
*Big Tree of Bunlahy*, by P. Colum. Macmillan.
*Glory of the Seas*, by A. Hewes. Knopf.
*Apprentices of Florence*, by A. Kyle. Houghton.

1935   DOBRY, by M. Shannon. Illustrated by A. Katchamakoff. Viking.
*The Pageant of Chinese History*, by E. Seeger. Longmans.
*Davy Crockett*, by C. Rourke. Harcourt.
*A Day on Skates*, by H. Van Stockum. Harper.

1936   CADDIE WOODLAWN, by C. R. Brink. Illustrated by K. Seredy.
  Macmillan.
*Honk the Moose*, by P. Stong. Dodd, Mead.
*The Good Master*, by K. Seredy. Viking.
*Young Walter Scott*, by E. J. Gray. Viking.
*All Sail Set*, by A. Sperry. Winston.

1937   ROLLER SKATES, by R. Sawyer. Illustrated by V. Angelo. Viking.
*Phoebe Fairchild: Her Book*, by L. Lenski. Stokes.
*Whistler's Van*, by I. Jones. Viking.
*The Golden Basket*, by L. Bemelmans. Viking.
*Winterbound*, by M. Bianco. Viking.
*Audubon*, by C. Rourke. Harcourt.
*The Codfish Musket*, by A. D. Hewes. Doubleday.

1938   THE WHITE STAG, by K. Seredy. Viking.
*Bright Island*, by M. L. Robinson. Random.
*Pecos Bill*, by J. C. Bowman. Little, Brown.
*On the Banks of Plum Creek*, by L. I. Wilder. Harper.

1939   THIMBLE SUMMER, by E. Enright. Rinehart.
*Leader by Destiny*, by J. Eaton. Harcourt.
*Penn*, by E. J. Gray. Viking.
*Nino*, by V. Angelo. Viking.
*"Hello, the Boat!"* by P. Crawford. Holt.
*Mr. Popper's Penguins*, by R. Atwater and F. Atwater. Little, Brown.

1940 DANIEL BOONE, by J. H. Daugherty. Viking.
*The Singing Tree*, by K. Seredy. Viking.
*Runner of the Mountain Tops*, by M. L. Robinson. Random.
*By the Shores of Silver Lake*, by L. I. Wilder. Harper.
*Boy With a Pack*, by S. W. Meader. Harcourt.

1941 CALL IT COURAGE, by A. Sperry. Macmillan.
*Blue Willow*, by D. Gates. Viking.
*Young Mac of Fort Vancouver*, by M. J. Carr. Harper.
*The Long Winter*, by L. I. Wilder. Harper.
*Nansen*, by A. G. Hall. Viking.

1942 THE MATCHLOCK GUN, by W. D. Edmonds. Illustrated by
        P. Lantz. Dodd, Mead.
*Little Town on the Prairie*, by L. I. Wilder. Harper.
*George Washington's World*, by G. Foster. Scribner's.
*Indian Captive*, by L. Lenski. Harper.
*Down Ryton Water*, by E. R. Gaggin. Viking.

1943 ADAM OF THE ROAD, by E. J. Gray. Illustrated by R. Lawson.
        Viking.
*The Middle Moffat*, by E. Estes. Harcourt.
*"Have You Seen Tom Thumb?"* by M. L. Hunt. Harper.

1944 JOHNNY TREMAIN, by E. Forbes. Illustrated by L. Ward.
        Houghton.
*These Happy Golden Years*, by L. I. Wilder. Harper.
*Fog Magic*, by J. L. Sauer. Viking.
*Rufus M.*, by E. Estes. Harcourt.
*Mountain Born*, by E. Yates. Coward-McCann.

1945 RABBIT HILL, by R. Lawson. Viking.
*The Hundred Dresses*, by E. Estes. Harcourt.
*The Silver Pencil*, by A. Dalgliesh. Scribner's.
*Abraham Lincoln's World*, by G. Foster. Scribner's.
*Lone Journey*, by J. Eaton. Harcourt.

1946 STRAWBERRY GIRL, by L. Lenski. Harper.
*Justin Morgan Had a Horse*, by M. Henry. Rand.
*The Moved-Outers*, by F. C. Means. Houghton.
*Blimsa, the Dancing Bear*, by C. Weston. Scribner's.
*New Found World*, by K. B. Shippen. Viking.

1947    MISS HICKORY, by C. S. Bailey. Illustrated by R. Gannett. Viking.
         *The Wonderful Year*, by N. Barnes. Messner.
         *Big Tree*, by M. Buff and C. Buff. Viking.
         *The Heavenly Tenants*, by W. Maxwell. Harper.
         *The Avion My Uncle Flew*, by C. Fisher. Appleton.
         *The Hidden Treasure of Glaston*, by E. M. Jewett. Viking.

1948    THE TWENTY-ONE BALLOONS, by W. Pène du Bois. Viking.
         *Pancakes-Paris*, by C. H. Bishop. Viking.
         *Li Lun, Lad of Courage*, by C. Treffinger. Abingdon.
         *The Quaint and Curious Quest of Johnny Longfoot*, by C. Besterman.
            Bobbs.
         *The Cow-Tail Switch*, by H. Courlander and G. Herzog. Holt.
         *Misty of Chincoteague*, by M. Henry. Rand.

1949    KING OF THE WIND, by M. Henry. Illustrated by
            W. Dennis. Rand.
         *Seabird*, by H. C. Holling. Houghton.
         *Daughter of the Mountains*, by L. Rankin. Viking.
         *My Father's Dragon*, by R. S. Gannett. Random.
         *Story of the Negro*, by A. Bontemps. Knopf.

1950    THE DOOR IN THE WALL, by M. de Angeli. Doubleday.
         *Tree of Freedom*, by R. Caudill. Viking.
         *Blue Cat of Castle Town*, by C. Coblentz. Longmans.
         *Kildee House*, by R. Montgomery. Doubleday.
         *George Washington*, by G. Foster. Scribner's.
         *Song of the Pines*, by W. Havighurst and M. Havighurst. Winston.

1951    AMOS FORTUNE, FREE MAN, by E. Yates. Illustrated by
            N. Unwin. Aladdin.
         *Better Known as Johnny Appleseed*, by M. L. Hunt. Harper.
         *Gandhi, Fighter Without a Sword*, by J. Eaton. Morrow.
         *Abraham Lincoln, Friend of the People*, by C. I. Judson. Follett.
         *The Story of Appleby Capple*, by A. Parrish. Harper.

1952    GINGER PYE, by E. Estes. Harcourt.
         *Americans Before Columbus*, by E. C. Baity. Viking.
         *Minn of the Mississippi*, by H. C. Holling. Houghton.
         *The Defender*, by N. Kalashnikoff. Scribner's.
         *The Light at Tern Rock*, by J. L. Sauer. Viking.
         *The Apple and the Arrow*, by M. Buff. Houghton.

1953    SECRET OF THE ANDES, by A. N. Clark. Illustrated by J. Charlot. Viking.
    *Charlotte's Web*, by E. B. White. Harper.
    *Moccasin Trail*, by E. J. McGraw. Coward-McCann.
    *Red Sails to Capri*, by A. Weil. Viking.
    *The Bears on Hemlock Mountain*, by A. Dalgliesh. Scribner's.
    *Birthdays of Freedom*, by G. Foster. Scribner's.

1954    AND NOW MIGUEL, by J. Krumgold. Illustrated by J. Charlot. Harper.
    *All Alone*, by C. H. Bishop. Viking
    *Shadrach*, by M. DeJong. Harper.
    *Hurry Home, Candy*, by M. DeJong. Harper.
    *Theodore Roosevelt, Fighting Patriot*, by C. I. Judson. Follett.
    *Magic Maize*, by M. Buff. Houghton.

1955    THE WHEEL ON THE SCHOOL, by M. DeJong. Illustrated by M. Sendak. Harper.
    *The Courage of Sarah Noble*, by A. Dalgliesh. Scribner's.
    *Banner in the Sky*, by J. R. Ullman. Harper.

1956    CARRY ON, MR. BOWDITCH, by J. L. Latham. Houghton.
    *The Golden Name Day*, by J. D. Lindquist. Harper.
    *The Secret River*, by M. K. Rawlings. Scribner's.
    *Men, Microscopes, and Living Things*, by K. B. Shippen. Viking.

1957    MIRACLES ON MAPLE HILL, by V. Sorensen. Illustrated by B. Krush and J. Krush. Harcourt.
    *Old Yeller*, by F. Gipson. Harper.
    *The House of Sixty Fathers*, by M. DeJong. Harper.
    *Mr. Justice Holmes*, by C. I. Judson. Follett.
    *The Corn Grows Ripe*, by D. Rhoads. Viking.
    *The Black Fox of Lorne*, by M. de Angeli. Doubleday.

1958    RIFLES FOR WATIE, by H. Keith. Illustrated by P. Burchard. Crowell.
    *The Horsecatcher*, by M. Sandoz. Westminster.
    *Gone-Away Lake*, by E. Enright. Harcourt.
    *The Great Wheel*, by R. Lawson. Viking.
    *Tom Paine, Freedom's Apostle*, by L. Gurko. Harper.

1959    THE WITCH OF BLACKBIRD POND, by E. G. Speare. Houghton.
    *The Family Under the Bridge*, by N. S. Carlson. Harper.
    *Along Came a Dog*, by M. DeJong. Harper.

*Chucaro*, by F. Kalnay. Harcourt.
*The Perilous Road*, by W. O. Steele. Harcourt.

1960 ONION JOHN, by J. Krumgold. Illustrated by S. Shimin. Harper.
*My Side of the Mountain*, by J. George. Dutton.
*America Is Born*, by G. Johnson. Morrow.
*The Gammage Cup*, by C. Kendall. Harcourt.

1961 ISLAND OF THE BLUE DOLPHINS, by S. O'Dell. Houghton.
*America Moves Forward*, by G. Johnson. Morrow.
*Old Ramon*, by J. Schaefer. Houghton.
*The Cricket in Times Square*, by G. Selden. Farrar, Straus & Giroux.

1962 THE BRONZE BOW, by E. G. Speare. Houghton.
*Frontier Living*, by E. Tunis. World.
*The Golden Goblet*, by E. J. McGraw. Coward-McCann.
*Belling the Tiger*, by M. Stolz. Harper.

1963 A WRINKLE IN TIME, by M. L'Engle. Farrar, Straus & Giroux.
*Thistle and Thyme*, by S. N. Leodhas. Holt.
*Men of Athens*, by O. Coolidge. Houghton.

1964 IT'S LIKE THIS, CAT, by E. Neville. Illustrated by E. Weiss. Harper.
*Rascal*, by S. North. Dutton.
*The Loner*, by E. Wier. McKay.

1965 SHADOW OF A BULL, by M. Wojciechowska. Illustrated by
    A. Smith. Atheneum.
*Across Five Aprils*, by I. Hunt. Follett.

1966 I, JUAN DE PAREJA, by E. B. de Trevino. Farrar, Straus, & Giroux.
*The Black Cauldron*, by L. Alexander. Holt.
*The Animal Family*, by R. Jarrell. Pantheon.
*The Noonday Friends*, by M. Stolz. Harper.

1967 UP A ROAD SLOWLY, by I. Hunt. Follett.
*The King's Fifth*, by S. O'Dell. Houghton.
*Zlatch the Goat and Other Stories*, by I. B. Singer. Harper.
*The Jazz Man*, by M. H. Weik. Atheneum.

1968 FROM THE MIXED-UP FILES OF MRS. BASIL E.
    FRANKWEILER, by E. L. Konigsburg. Atheneum.
*Jennifer, Hecate, Macbeth, William McKinley, and Me, Elizabeth*, by
    E. L. Konigsburg. Atheneum.

*The Black Pearl*, by S. O'Dell. Houghton.
*The Fearsome Inn*, by I. B. Singer. Scribner's.
*The Egypt Game*, by Z. K. Snyder. Atheneum.

1969   THE HIGH KING, by L. Alexander. Holt.
*To Be a Slave*, by J. Lester. Dial.
*When Shlemiel Went to Warsaw and Other Stories*, by I. B. Singer.
   Farrar, Straus, & Giroux.

1970   SOUNDER, by W. H. Armstrong. Harper.
*Our Eddie*, by S. Ish-Kishor. Pantheon.
*The Many Ways of Seeing: An Introduction to the Pleasures of Art*, by
   J. G. Moore. World.
*Journey Outside*, by M. Q. Steele. Viking.

1971   SUMMER OF THE SWANS, by B. Byars. Viking.
*Kneeknock Rise*, by N. Babbitt. Farrar, Straus & Giroux.
*Enchantress from the Stars*, by S. L. Engdahl. Atheneum.
*Sing Down the Moon*, by S. O'Dell. Houghton.

1972   MRS. FRISBY AND THE RATS OF NIMH, by R. C. O'Brien.
   Atheneum.
*Incident at Hawk's Hill*, by A. W. Eckert. Little, Brown.
*The Planet of Junior Brown*, by V. Hamilton. Macmillan.
*The Tombs of Atuan*, by U. K. LeGuin. Atheneum.
*Annie and the Old One*, by M. Miles. Little, Atlantic.
*The Headless Cupid*, by Z. K. Snyder. Atheneum.

1973   JULIE OF THE WOLVES, by J. C. George. Harper.
*Frog and Toad Together*, by A. Lobel. Harper.
*The Upstairs Room*, by J. Reiss. Harper.
*The Witches of Worm*, by Z. K. Snyder. Atheneum.

1974   THE SLAVE DANCER, by P. Fox. Bradbury.
*The Dark Is Rising*, by S. Cooper. Atheneum. McElderry.

1975   M. C. HIGGINS THE GREAT, by V. Hamilton. Macmillan.
*My Brother Sam Is Dead*, by J. Collier and C. Collier. Four Winds.
*Philip Hall Likes Me. I Reckon Maybe*, by B. Greene. Dial.
*The Perilous Guard*, by E. Pope. Houghton.
*Figgs & Phantoms*, by E. Raskin. Dutton.

1976   THE GREY KING, by S. Cooper. Atheneum, McElderry.
*Dragonwings*, by L. Yep. Harper.
*The Hundred Penny Box*, by S. Mathis. Viking.

1977   ROLL OF THUNDER, HEAR MY CRY, by M. D. Taylor. Dial.
*Abel's Island*, by W. Steig. Farrar, Straus & Giroux.
*A String in the Harp*, by N. Bond. McElderry.

1978   BRIDGE TO TERABITHIA, by K. Paterson. Harper.
*Anpao: An American Indian Odyssey*, by J. Highwater. Harper.
*Ramona and Her Father*, by B. Cleary. Morrow.

1979   THE WESTING GAME, by E. Raskin. Dutton.
*The Great Gilly Hopkins*, by K. Paterson. Harper.

1980   A GATHERING OF DAYS: A NEW ENGLAND GIRL'S
JOURNAL, 1830–32, by J. W. Blos. Scribner's.
*The Road from Home: The Story of an Armenian Girl*, by D. Kherdian.
Greenwillow.

1981   JACOB HAVE I LOVED, by K. Paterson. Harper.
*The Fledgling*, by J. Langton. Harper.
*Ring of Endless Light*, by M. L'Engle. Farrar, Straus & Giroux.

1982   A VISIT TO WILLIAM BLAKE'S INN: POEMS FOR INNOCENT
AND EXPERIENCED TRAVELERS, by N. Willard. Illustrated
by A. Provensen and M. Provensen. Harcourt.
*Ramona Quimby, Age 8*, by B. Cleary. Morrow.
*Upon the Head of the Goat: A Childhook in Hungary, 1939–1944*, by
A. Siegal. Farrar, Straus & Giroux.

1983   DICEY'S SONG, by C. Voigt. Atheneum.
*The Blue Sword*, by R. McKinley. Greenwillow.
*Doctor De Soto*, by W. Steig. Farrar, Straus & Giroux.
*Graven Images*, by P. Fleischman. Harper.
*Homesick: My Own Story*, by J. Fritz. Putnam.
*Sweet Whispers, Brother Rush*, by V. Hamilton. Philomel.

1984   DEAR MR. HENSHAW, by B. Cleary. Morrow.
*The Wish Giver*, by B. Brittain. Harper.
*A Solitary Blue*, by C. Voigt. Atheneum.
*The Sign of the Beaver*, by E. G. Speare. Houghton.
*Sugaring Time*, by K. Lasky. Macmillan.

1985    THE HERO AND THE CROWN, by R. McKinley. Greenwillow.
*The Moves Make the Man*, by B. Brooks. Harper.
*One-Eyed Cat*, by P. Fox. Bradbury.
*Like Jake and Me*, by M. Jukes. Illustrated by L. Bloom. Knopf.

1986    SARAH, PLAIN AND TALL, by P. MacLachlan. Harper.
*Commodore Perry in the Land of the Shogun*, by R. Blumberg. Lothrop.
*Dogsong*, by G. Paulsen. Bradbury.

1987    THE WHIPPING BOY, by S. Fleischman. Greenwillow.
*A Fine White Dust*, by C. Rylant. Bradbury.
*On My Honor*, by M. D. Bauer. Clarion.
*Volcano*, by P. Lauber. Bradbury.

1988    LINCOLN: A PHOTOBIOGRAPHY, by R. Freedman. Clarion.
*After the Rain*, by N. F. Mazer. Morrow.
*Hatchet*, by G. Paulsen. Bradbury.

1989    JOYFUL NOISE: POEMS FOR TWO VOICES, by P. Fleischman.
Harper.
*In the Beginning: Creation Stories from Around the World*, by V. Hamilton.
Harcourt.
*Scorpions*, by W. D. Myers. Harper.

1990    NUMBER THE STARS, by L. Lowry. Houghton.
*Afternoon of the Elves*, by J. T. Lisle. Orchard.
*Shabanu: Daughter of the Wind*, by S. F. Staples. Knopf.
*The Winter Room*, by G. Paulsen. Orchard.

1991    MANIAC MAGEE, by J. Spinelli. Little, Brown.
*The True Confessions of Charlotte Doyle*, by Avi. Orchard.

1992    SHILOH, by P. R. Naylor. Atheneum.
*Nothing but the Truth*, by Avi. Orchard.
*The Wright Brothers*, by R. Freedman. Holiday.

1993    MISSING MAY, by C. Rylant. Orchard.
*What Hearts*, by B. Brooks. Harper.
*The Dark-Thirty: Southern Tales of the Supernatural*, by P. McKissack.
Illustrated by B. Pinkney. Knopf.
*Somewhere in the Darkness*, by W. D. Myers. Scholastic.

1994    THE GIVER, by L. Lowry. Houghton.
*Crazy Lady!* by J. L. Conly. Harper.

*Eleanor Roosevelt: A Life of Discovery*, by R. Freedman. Clarion.
*Dragon's Gate*, by L. Yep. Harper.

1995   WALK TWO MOONS, by S. Creech. Harper.
*Catherine, Called Birdy*, by K. Cushman. Clarion.
*The Ear, the Eye and the Arm*, by N. Farmer. Orchard.

1996   THE MIDWIFE'S APPRENTICE, by K. Cushman. Clarion.
*What Jamie Saw*, by C. Coman. Front Street.
*The Watsons Go to Birmingham—1963*, by C. P. Curtis. Delacorte.
*Yolonda's Genius*, by C. Fenner. McElderry.
*The Great Fire*, by J. Murphy. Scholastic.

1997   THE VIEW FROM SATURDAY, by E. L. Konigsburg.
    Karl/Atheneum.
*A Girl Named Disaster*, by N. Farmer. Jackson/Orchard.
*The Moorchild*, by E. McGraw. McElderry.
*The Thief*, by M. W. Turner. Greenwillow.
*Belle Prater's Boy*, by R. White. Farrar, Straus & Giroux.

1998   OUT OF THE DUST, by K. Hesse. Scholastic.
*Lily's Crossing*, by P. R. Giff. Delacorte.
*Ella Enchanted*, by G. C. Levine. HarperCollins.
*Wringer*, by J. Spinella. HarperCollins.

1999   HOLES, by L. Sachar. Farrar, Straus & Giroux.
*A Long Way from Chicago*, by R. Peck. Dial.

2000   BUD, NOT BUDDY, by C. P. Curtis. Delacorte Press.
*Getting Near to Baby*, by A. Couloumbis. G. P. Putnam's Sons.
*26 Fairmont Avenue*, by T. de Paola. G. P. Putnam's Sons.
*Our Only May Amelia*, by J. L. Holm. HarperCollins.

APPENDIX C

# Literature Cited
# in the Lesson Plans

Akass, S. (1995). *Swim, number nine duckling*. Honesdale, PA: Boyds Mills.

Alborough, J. (1997). *Watch out! Big Bro's coming!* Cambridge, MA: Candlewick Press.

Alphin, E. M. (1991). *The ghost cadet*. New York: Scholastic.

Archambault, J., & Martin, B. Jr. (1994). *A beautiful feast for a big king cat*. New York: HarperCollins.

Bagert, B. (1992). *Let me be . . . the boss*. Honesdale, PA: Boyds Mills/Wordsong.

Bemelmans, L. (1939, 1962). *Madeline*. New York: Viking.

Blain, D. (1991). *Boxcar children cookbook*. Morton Grove, IL: Whitman.

Brett, J. (1985). *Annie and the wild animals*. Boston: Houghton Mifflin.

Carle, E. (1969). *The very hungry caterpillar*. New York: Philomel.

Cauley, L. B. (1982). *The lock, the mouse, and the little red hen*. New York: Putnam.

Cauley, L. B. (1988). *The trouble with Tyrannosaurus Rex*. San Diego: Harcourt Brace.

Christopher, M. (1954). *The lucky baseball bat*. Boston: Little, Brown.

Christopher, M. (1964). *Catcher with a glass arm*. Boston: Little, Brown.

Clements, A. (1996). *Frindle*. New York: Simon & Schuster.

Climo, S. (1989). *The Egyptian Cinderella*. New York: HarperCollins.

Climo, S. (1993). *The Korean Cinderella*. New York: HarperCollins.

Collodi, C. (Translator E. Harden). (1988). *The adventures of Pinocchio*. New York: Knopf.

Cormier, R. (1979). *After the first death*. New York: Pantheon.

Cousteau Society. (1991). *An adventure in the Amazon*. New York: Simon & Schuster.

Creech, S. (1994). *Walk two moons.* New York: Harper Trophy.

de Paola, T. (1978). *Pancakes for breakfast.* San Diego: Harcourt.

de Paola, T. (Reteller). (1988). *The legend of the Indian paintbrush.* New York: Putnam.

Fenner, C. (1995). *Yolanda's genius.* New York: Aladdin.

Fleischman, P. (1986). *I am Phoenix: Poems for two voices.* New York: Harper.

Fleischman, P. (1988). *Joyful noise: Poems for two voices.* New York: Harper.

Fleischman, S. (1977). *Me and the man on the moon-eyed horse.* Boston: Little, Brown.

Fleming, D. (1994). *Barnyard banter.* New York: Holt.

Galdone, P. (1971). *Three Aesop fox fables.* New York: Clarion.

Geisel, T. S. (Dr. Seuss). (1987). *Fox in socks.* New York: Random Library.

Guarino, D. (1989). *Is your mama a llama?* New York: Scholastic.

Guilfoile, E. (1962). *The house that Jack built.* New York: Holt, Rinehart, & Winston.

Harrison, D. L. (1992). *Somebody catch my homework.* Honesdale, PA: Boyds Mills/Wordsong.

Haskins, J. (1995). *The day Fort Sumter was fired on: A photo history of the Civil War.* New York: Scholastic.

Henkes, K. (1991). *Chrysanthemum.* New York: Greenwillow.

Hoban, T. (1995). *Colors everywhere.* New York: Greenwillow.

Hooks, W. H. (1998). *Pioneer cat.* New York: Random House.

Julivert, M. A. (1994). *The fascinating world of . . . bats.* New York: Barron's Educational Services.

Juster, N. (1989). *The phantom tollbooth.* New York: Knopf.

Katzen, M., & Henderson, A. (1994). *Pretend soup and other real recipes: A cookbook for preschoolers and up.* Berkeley, CA: Tricycle.

Lisker, T. (1977). *Terror in the tropics: The army ants.* New York: Contemporary Perspectives.

Lowry, L. (1993). *The giver.* Boston: Houghton Mifflin.

McGovern, A. (1971). *Stone soup.* New York: Scholastic.

McKellar, S. (1993). *Counting rhymes.* New York: Dorling.

Maclean, N. (1976). *A river runs through it and other stories.* New York: Pocket Books.

Martin, B., Jr. (1964, 1992). *Brown bear, brown bear, what do you see?* New York: Holt.

Martin, B., Jr. (1991). *Polar bear, polar bear, what do you hear?* New York: Holt.

Martin, B., Jr., & Archambault, J. (1985). *The ghost-eye tree.* New York: Holt.

Martin, B., Jr., & Archambault, J. (1989). *Chicka chicka boom boom.* New York: Simon & Schuster.

Marzollo, J. (1990). *Pretend you're a cat.* New York: Dial.

Mullins, P. (1993). *Dinosaur encore.* New York: HarperCollins/Putnam.

Neitzel, S. (1989). *The jacket I wear in the snow.* New York: Greenwillow.

Ness, E. (1966). *Sam, Bangs, and moonshine.* New York: Holt.

Nixon, J. L. (1988). *If you were a writer.* New York: Simon & Schuster.

Nomaska, J. (1985). *Busy Monday morning.* New York: Greenwillow.

Olaleye, I. (1995). *The distant talking drum*. Honesdale, PA: Boyds Mills/ Wordsong.

O'Neal, J. (Compiler). (1993). *Blues masters* (Cassette Recording No. R471128). Los Angeles: Rhino.

Ormerod, J. (1981). *Moonlight*. New York: Lothrop.

Osborne, M. (1995). *Magic tree house #6: Afternoon on the Amazon*. New York: Scholastic.

Paulsen, G. (1987). *Hatchet*. New York: Bradbury.

Peek, M. (1981). *Roll over!* Boston: Houghton Mifflin.

Priceman, M. (1994). *How to make an apple pie and see the world*. New York: Knopf.

Raskin, E. (1978). *The Westing game*. New York: Dutton.

Rawls, W. (1961). *Where the red fern grows*. New York: Doubleday.

Redford, R. (Director). (1992). *A river runs through it* [Videotape]. (Available from Columbia TriStar Home Video, Los Angeles, CA)

Rood, R. (1993). *Tide pools*. New York: Harper Trophy.

Sachar, L. (1998). *Holes*. Farrar, Straus & Giroux.

San Souci, R. D. (1978). *The legend of Scarface: A Blackfeet Indian tale*. Garden City, NY: Doubleday.

Sendak, M. (1963). *Where the wild things are*. New York: Harper.

Smith, R. K. (1989). *Bobby Baseball*. New York: Delacorte.

Sobol, D. J. (1979). *Encyclopedia Brown, boy detective*. New York: Bantam.

*Sports illustrated for kids*. Birmingham, AL: Time Magazine.

Stuart, G. E., & Stuart, G. S. (1977). *The mysterious Maya*. Washington, DC: National Geographic Society.

Thayer, E. (1888, 1989). *Casey at the bat*. New York: Putnam.

Van Allsburg, C. (1981). *Jumanji*. Boston: Houghton Mifflin.

Van Allsburg, C. (1987). *The z was zapped*. Boston: Houghton Mifflin.

Vass, G. (1979). *Reggie Jackson*. Chicago: Children's Press.

Viorst, J. (1976). *Alexander and the terrible, horrible, no good, very bad day*. New York: Atheneum.

Waddell, M. (1992). *Owl babies*. New York: Candlewick Press.

White, E. B. (1952). *Charlotte's web*. New York: Harper & Row.

Williams, M. (1922). *The velveteen rabbit*. New York: Doubleday.

Williams, R. (Reader). (1995). *Jumanji* [Cassette Recording]. Boston: Houghton Mifflin.

Winthrop, E. (1985). *Castle in the attic*. New York: Putnam.

APPENDIX D

# *Professional Resources*

Armento, B. J. (1977). Teacher behaviors related to student achievement on a social science concept test. *Journal of Teacher Education, 28,* 46–52.

Bormuth, J. R. (1975). The cloze procedure: Literacy in the classroom. In W. D. Page (Ed.), *Help for the reading teacher: New directions in research* (pp. 60–90). Urbana, IL: ERIC Clearinghouse on Reading and Communication Skills.

Braunger, J., & Lewis, J. P. (1997). *Building a knowledge base in reading.* Portland, OR: Northwest Regional Educational Laboratory; Urbana, IL: National Council of Teachers of English; Newark, DE: International Reading Association.

Clay, M. M. (1991). *Becoming literate: The construction of inner control.* Portsmouth, NH: Heineman.

Cullinan, B. E., & Galda, L. (1998). *Literature and the child* (4th ed.). Fort Worth, TX: Harcourt Brace.

Davis, F. B. (1944). Fundamental factors of comprehension in reading. *Psychometrika, 9,* 185–197.

Freedman, G., & Reynolds, E. G. (1980). Enriching basal reader lessons with semantic webbing. *The Reading Teacher, 34,* 677–684.

Gardner, H. (1983). *Frames of mind: The theory of multiple intelligences.* New York: Basic Books.

Gardner, H. (1996). *MI: Intelligence, understanding, and the mind* [Video]. (Available from Into the Classroom Media, 10573 West Pico Blvd. #162, Los Angeles, CA 90064)

Gere, A. R. (1985). *Roots in the sawdust: Writing to learn across the disciplines.* Urbana, IL: National Council of Teachers of English.

Gipe, J. P. (1998). *Multiple paths to literacy: Corrective techniques for classroom teachers* (4th ed.). Upper Saddle River, NJ: Prentice-Hall.

Gunning, T. G. (2000). *Creating literacy instruction for all children* (3rd ed.). Boston: Allyn & Bacon.

Gunter, M. A., Estes, T. H., & Schwab, J. H. (1990). *Instruction: A models approach.* Boston: Allyn & Bacon.

Huey, E. B. (1973). *The psychology and pedagogy of reading.* Cambridge, MA: MIT Press. (First published in 1908 by Macmillan)

Jalongo, M., Twiest, M. M., & Gerlach, G. (1999). *The college learner: Reading, studying, and attaining academic success* (2nd ed.). Columbus, OH: Merrill/Prentice Hall.

Leu, D. J., & Kinzer, C. K. (1999). *Effective literacy instruction, K–8* (4th ed.). Upper Saddle River, NJ: Prentice-Hall.

Lundquist, J. K. (1989). *English from the roots up.* Bellevue, WA: Literacy Unlimited.

Manzo, A. V. (1969). The ReQuest Procedure. *Journal of Reading, 13,* 123–126.

McCracken, R. A. (1971). Initiating drop everything and read. *Journal of Reading, 14,* 521–524, 582–583.

Montague, E. J. (1987). *Fundamentals of secondary classroom instruction.* Columbus, OH: Merrill.

Ogle, D. M. (1986). A teaching model that develops active reading of expository text. *The Reading Teacher, 39,* 564–570.

Orlich, D. C., Harder, R. J., Callahan, R. C., & Gibson, H. W. (1998). *Teaching strategies: A guide to better instruction* (5th ed.). Boston: Houghton Mifflin.

Professional Standards and Ethics Committee. (1998). *Standards for reading professionals* (Rev. ed.). Newark, DE: International Reading Association.

Robinson, F. P. (1961). *Effective study* (Rev. ed.). New York: Harper & Brothers.

Samuels, S. J. (1981). Some essentials of decoding. *Exceptional Education Quarterly, 2,* 11–25.

Scarborough, H. S. (1991). Early syntactic development of dyslexic children. *Annals of Dyslexia, 41,* 207–220.

Shapiro, B. K., Palmer, F. B., Antell, S., Bilker, S., Ross, A., & Capute, A. J. (1990). Precursors of reading delay: Neurodevelopmental milestones. *Pediatrics, 85,* 416–420.

Simpson, M. L. (1986). PORPE: A writing strategy for studying and learning in the content areas. *Journal of Reading, 29,* 407–414.

Sloyer, S. (1982). *Readers theatre: Story dramatization in the classroom.* Urbana, IL: National Council of Teachers of English.

Snow, C. E., Burns, M. S., & Griffin, P. (Eds.). (1998). *Preventing reading difficulties in young children.* Washington, DC: National Academy Press.

Strickland, E. (1975, October). Assignment mastery. *Reading World,* 25–31.

Vacca, R. T., & Vacca, J. L. (1999). *Content area reading: Literacy and learning across the curriculum* (6th ed.). New York: Longman.

Walker, B. J. (1992). *Diagnostic teaching of reading: Techniques for instruction and assessment.* New York: Macmillan.

Walker, D., Greenwood, C., Hart, B., & Carta, J. (1994). Prediction of school outcomes based on socioeconomic status and early language production. *Child Development, 65,*606–621.

Wright, C. J., & Nuthall, G. (1970). Relationships between teacher behaviors and pupil achievement in three experimental science lessons. *American Educational Research Journal,* 7, 477–491.

Zeno, S. M., Ivens, S. H., Millard, R. T., & Duvvuri, R. (1995). *The educator's word frequency guide.* Brewster, NY: Touchstone Applied Science Associates.

APPENDIX E

# *Internet Sites Related to Literacy*

American Library Association (ALA). <http://www.ala.org/> Provides leadership in defending intellectual freedom and promotes high-quality library and information services.

Center for the Improvement of Early Reading Achievement (CIERA). <http://www.ciera.org/> Supports the improvement of reading achievement of America's children by disseminating theoretical, empirical, and practical solutions to learning and teaching of beginning reading.

Children's Book Council. <http://www.cbcbooks.org/> Provides resources to be used by parents, caregivers, teachers, and librarians.

Children's Literature Web Guide. <http://www.acs.ucalgary.ca/~dkbrown/> Provides a categorized collection of Internet resources related to books for children and young adults.

ERIC Clearinghouse on Reading, English, and Communication (ERIC/REC). <http://www.indiana.edu/~eric_rec/> Provides a variety of materials and links to extensive literacy-related resources.

International Reading Association (IRA). <http://www.reading.org/> Serves as a clearinghouse for the dissemination of reading research through conferences, journals, and other publications.

National Association for Bilingual Education (NABE). <http://www.nabe.org/> Addresses the educational needs of language-minority student in the United States and advances language competencies and multicultural understanding.

National Council of Teachers of English (NCTE). <http://www.ncte.org/> Promotes improving the teaching of English and the language arts.

National Information Center for Children and Youth with Disabilities (NICHCY). <http://www.nichcy.org/> Provides information on disabilities and disability-related issues for families, educators, and professionals, with a special focus on children and youth.

Regional Educational Laboratories. <http://www.nwrel.org/national/> Coordinates the regional educational laboratory involvement in the America Reads Challenge and literacy initiatives.

U.S. Department of Education. <http://www.ed.gov/> Supports communities and schools in literacy work and includes the America Reads Challenge.

# *Index*

*Note:* Worksheets and sample figures are indicated by *italic* page numbers.